SELF SERVICE REPORTING IN DYNAMICS AX 2012 USING EXCEL AND POWER BI

Second Edition

Murray Fife

ISBN-13: 978-1519143891

ISBN-10: 1519143893

Preface

What You Need For This Guide

All the examples shown in this blueprint were done with the Microsoft Dynamics AX 2012 virtual machine image that was downloaded from the Microsoft CustomerSource or PartnerSource site. If you don't have your own installation of Microsoft Dynamics AX 2012, you can also use the images found on the Microsoft Learning Download Center or deployed through Lifecycle Services. The following list of software from the virtual image was leveraged within this guide:

Microsoft Dynamics AX 2012 R3 CU9

Even though all the preceding software was used during the development and testing of the recipes in this book, they may also work on earlier versions of the software with minor tweaks and adjustments, and should also work on later versions without any changes.

Errata

Although we have taken every care to ensure the accuracy of our content, mistakes do happen. If you find a mistake in one of our books—maybe a mistake in the text or the code—we would be grateful if you would report this to us. By doing so, you can save other readers from frustration and help us improve subsequent versions of this book. If you find any errata, please report them by emailing editor@blindsquirrelpublishing.com.

Piracy

Piracy of copyright material on the Internet is an ongoing problem across all media. If you come across any illegal copies of our works, in any form, on the Internet, please provide us with the location address or website name immediately so that we can pursue a remedy.

Please contact us at legal@blindsquirrelpublishing.com with a link to the suspected pirated material.

We appreciate your help in protecting our authors, and our ability to bring you valuable content.

Questions

You can contact us at help@blindsquirrelpublishing.com if you are having a problem with any aspect of the book, and we will do our best to address it.

Table of Contents

daxc
www.dynamicsaxcompanions.com
Dynamics AX Companions
- 3 -
www.blindsquirrelpublishing.com
© 2015 Blind Squirrel Publishing, LLC , All Rights Reserved
BLIND SQUIRREL
PUBLISHING

daxc
www.dynamicsaxcompanions.com
Dynamics AX Companions
- 4 -
www.blindsquirrelpublishing.com
© 2015 Blind Squirrel Publishing, LLC , All Rights Reserved

BLIND SQUIRREL
PUBLISHING

INTRODUCTION

Having users perform their own reporting has been a dream on both sides of the organization. The IT group don't particularly like creating reports for the users when they could be spending their time on cooler projects, and users don't particularly like waiting for IT to create the reports that they need to track the data because it's never quite what they wanted, and also takes so long to get (because of the first reason) that it's usually out-of-date. If only there was a solution...

Well there is, because there are so many tools built into Dynamics AX and also the productivity tools like Excel and Word that the users can easily create their own reports themselves without having to get the IT group involved. Everybody wins!

In this guide we will show you how the users can do just that, it's so easy that they may not even realize that they are creating reports.

SELF SERVICE REPORTING USING EXCEL AND POWER BI

When people first think of reporting, they generally think about the old fashioned reports that they are used to requesting from the IT department which are probably created through some reporting tool like SQL Server Reporting Services. And although there are a lot of those reports available within Dynamics AX out of the box, they are not really reports that the end users are able to modify, and they are very rigid in their formatting.

Something that people don't think about is that the forms that they are using every day are the best reports that are out there, and they can change them any time that they like. List pages give you a wealth of information that is filterable and then you can save away the view for reference later on giving you a quick and easy way to analyze your data.

Additionally, all of this information is exportable to Excel, creating a refreshable (and secure) worksheet with the data directly from Dynamics AX. Once you have the data in Excel there is no end wo what you can do with it, from creating pivot table to creating PowerView dashboards. These are all things that the users have been doing for years but refreshing the data has been a chore. Not anymore.

Finally, the users can create their own dashboards using the Analyze option that will create web based PowerView dashboards. These are even more powerful because they link to the cubes within Dynamics AX and allow the users to then convert them over to interactive PowerPoints at the click of a button.

All these reporting options are so natural for the user, they may not even realize that what they are doing is really impressive. It's just Excel.

In this chapter we will explore some of the reporting options that the users can take advantage of themselves using the tools that are so near and dear to their hearts already.

Using List Pages as User Reports

The first thing that we will highlight is that the Dynamics AX list pages are the best reporting options that is there for the user. The list pages can be rearranged, filtered, have fields added to them, sorted and a whole slew of other personalization options making it the perfect way to review data.

daxc
www.dynamicsaxcompanions.com
Dynamics AX Companions
- 9 -
www.blindsquirrelpublishing.com
© 2015 Blind Squirrel Publishing, LLC , All Rights Reserved

BLIND SQUIRREL
PUBLISHING

Step By Step Walkthrough

Using List Pages as User Reports

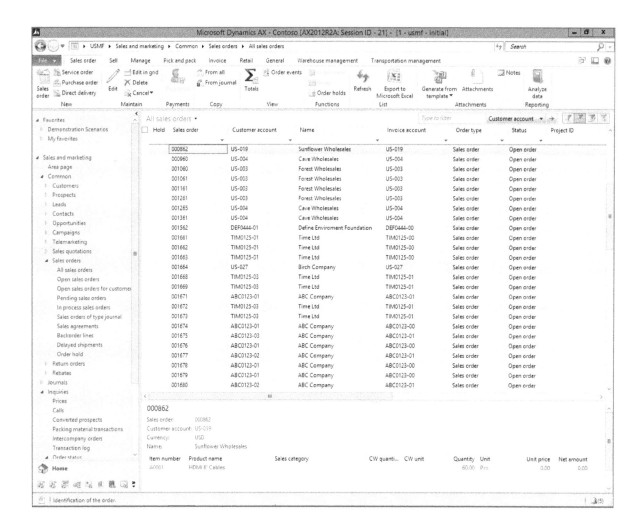

For example, if you open up the **All Sales Orders** list page then you will see all of the common information that the user may need in a report of open sales orders.

Step By Step Walkthrough

Using List Pages as User Reports

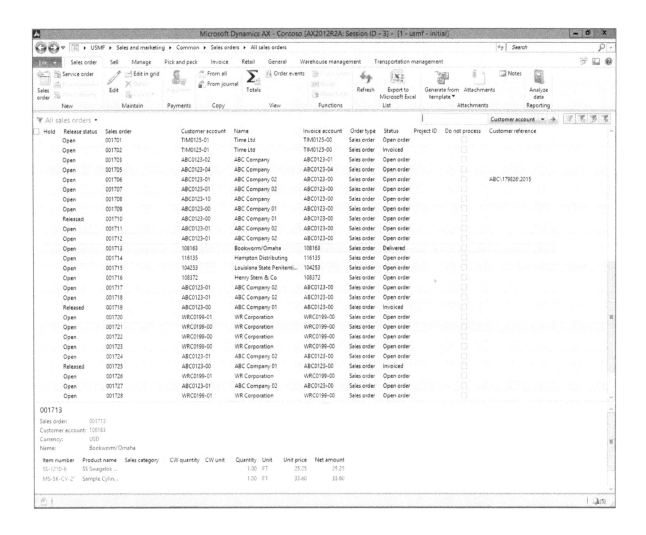

If the user needs to re-arrange any of the fields, then they can just drag and drop the fields around in the list page. For example, here we moved the **Release Status** to the left side of the list page.

Step By Step Walkthrough

Using List Pages as User Reports

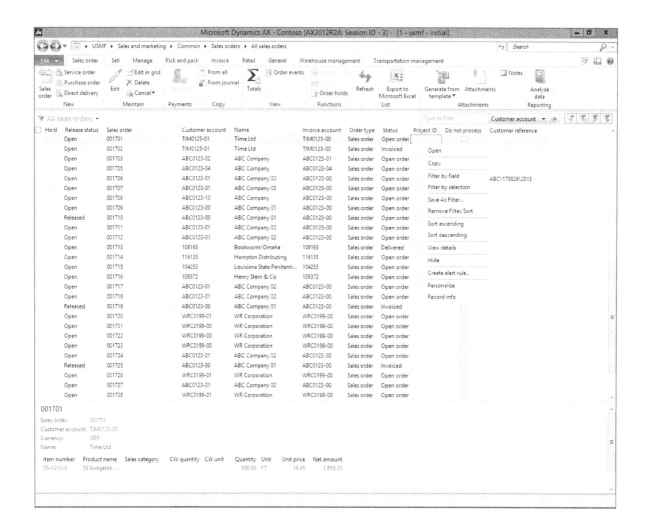

If there are fields that the use does not need to see, then they can just right-mouse-click on the field and then select the **Hide** option from the context menu that pops up.

daxc   www.dynamicsaxcompanions.com
Dynamics AX Companions
- 12 -
www.blindsquirrelpublishing.com
© 2015 Blind Squirrel Publishing, LLC, All Rights Reserved
BLIND SQUIRREL
PUBLISHING

Step By Step Walkthrough

Using List Pages as User Reports

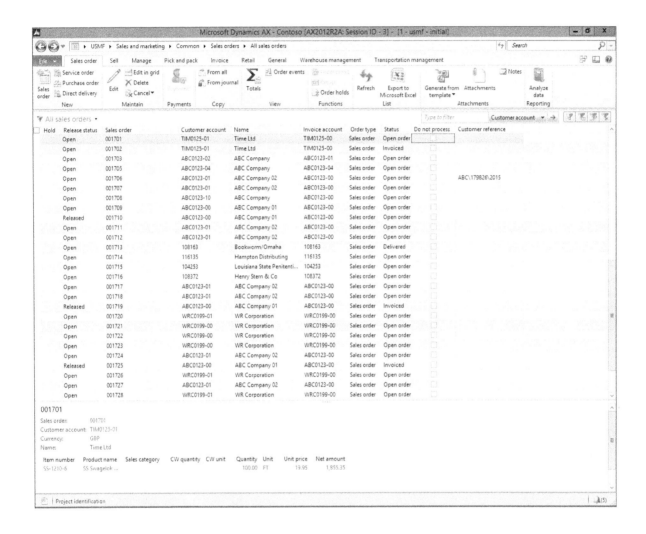

Then the field is hidden from the view.

If the users are just looking for a way to view data from Dynamics AX, then there is no reason why they should have to resort to having to create custom reports. All of the information is available on the list pages themselves and the user has the ability to even rearrange the data and also hide information that they are not interested in. I's the ideal first line of attack when it comes to self-service reporting.

Use Edit in Grid as your Reporting Worksheet

Additionally, most of the list pages within Dynamics AX have a second version which is called the **Edit In Grid** view. This is a great way to have a master reporting form for the users and not clutter up the main list page with the extra fields that they may need to report off.

daxc
www.dynamicsaxcompanions.com
Dynamics AX Companions
- 15 -
www.blindsquirrelpublishing.com
© 2015 Blind Squirrel Publishing, LLC , All Rights Reserved
BLIND SQUIRREL
PUBLISHING

Step By Step Walkthrough

Use Edit in Grid as your Reporting Worksheet

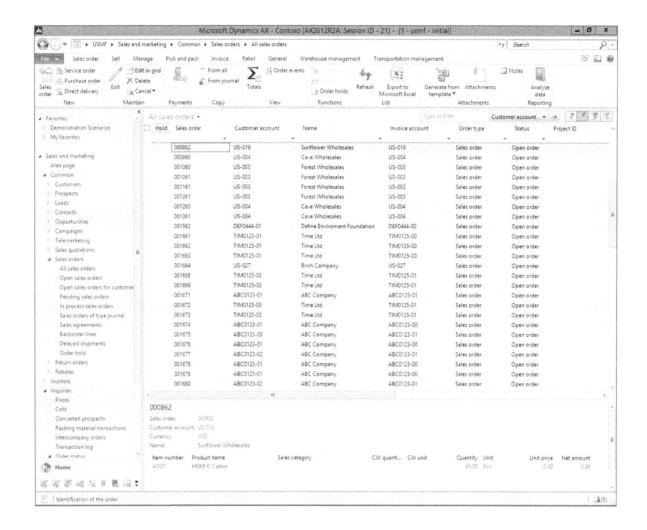

To access the **Edit In Grid** view within the **All Sales Orders** view, just click on the **Edit In Grid** button within the **Maintain** group of the **Sales Order** ribbon bar.

daxc
www.dynamicsaxcompanions.com
Dynamics AX Companions
- 16 -
www.blindsquirrelpublishing.com
© 2015 Blind Squirrel Publishing, LLC , All Rights Reserved
BLIND SQUIRREL
PUBLISHING

Step By Step Walkthrough

Use Edit in Grid as your Reporting Worksheet

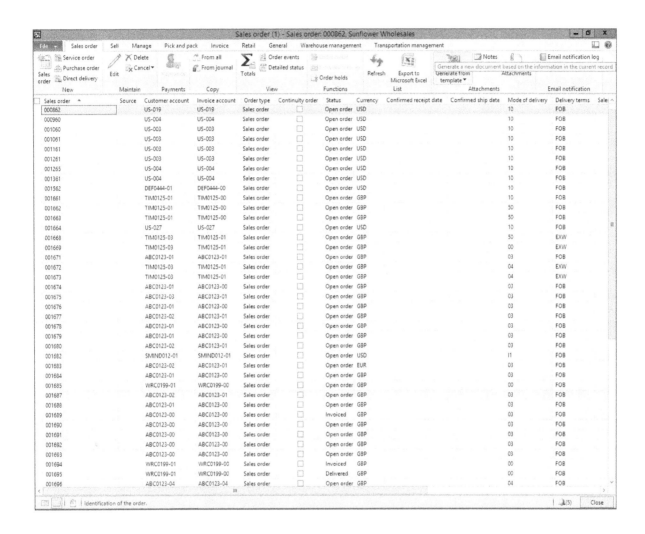

This will open up a new grid form that shows you a little more information.

Using the Edit In Grid view is like a list page behind the list pages, and it's great to know that it's there. You can keep the main list page clean with just the information that you need to find things on a day to day basis, but use the Edit In Grid view as your reporting worksheet.

Adding Additional Fields to List Page Views

One of the benefits of the list pages within Dynamics AX is that you can add additional fields to the views, so if there is something that you need for reporting and analysis that isn't currently on the form then all you need to do is add it.

Step By Step Walkthrough

Adding Additional Fields to List Page Views

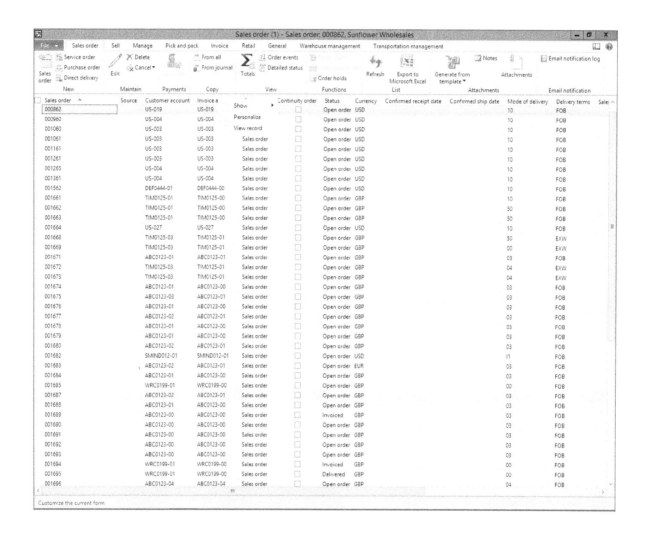

To do this, just right-mouse-click on the data within the list page, or the heading in the list page and then click on the Personalize option.

Step By Step Walkthrough

Adding Additional Fields to List Page Views

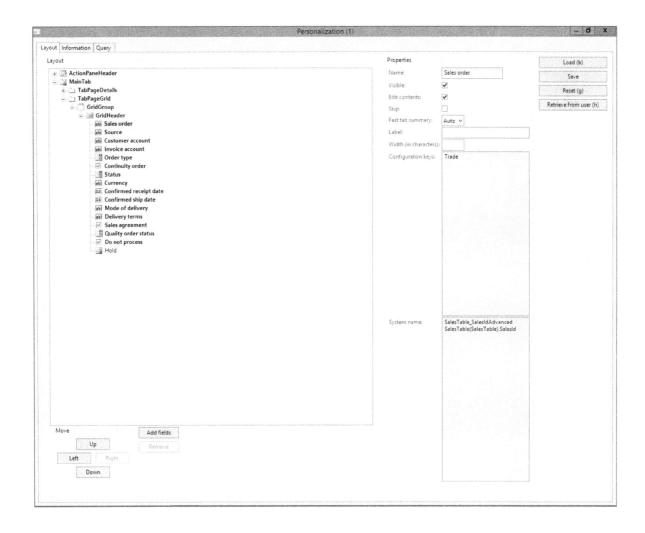

This will open up the Personalization form and you will be able to see all of the fields that are currently displayed within the list page. To add a new field all you need to do is click on the Add Fields button.

daxc
www.dynamicsaxcompanions.com
Dynamics AX Companions
- 21 -
www.blindsquirrelpublishing.com
© 2015 Blind Squirrel Publishing, LLC , All Rights Reserved

BLIND SQUIRREL
PUBLISHING

Step By Step Walkthrough

Adding Additional Fields to List Page Views

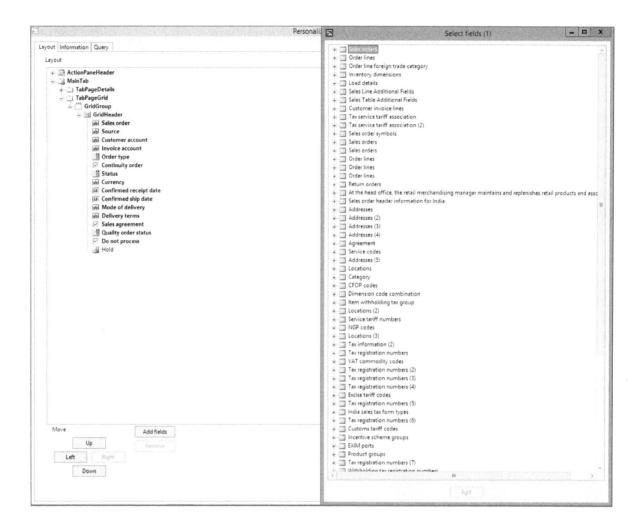

This will open up the Field Explorer and you will be able to see all of the fields that are associated with the form and also any related tables as well.

Step By Step Walkthrough

Adding Additional Fields to List Page Views

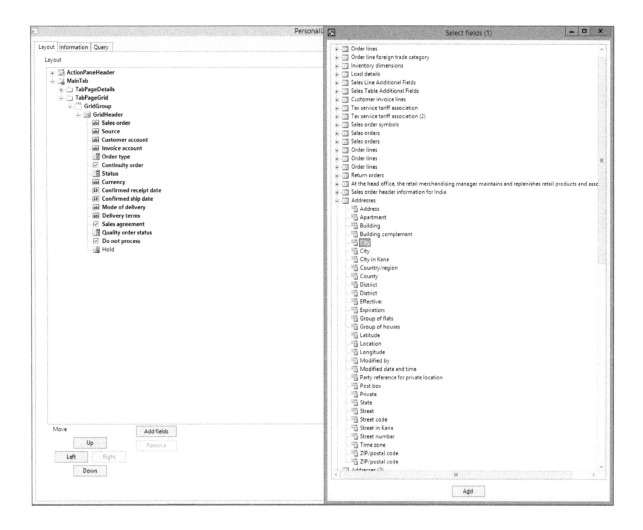

If you expand out the Addresses field group then you will see all of the address fields that are related to the Sales Orders.

daxc
www.dynamicsaxcompanions.com
Dynamics AX Companions
- 23 -
www.blindsquirrelpublishing.com
© 2015 Blind Squirrel Publishing, LLC , All Rights Reserved
BLIND SQUIRREL
PUBLISHING

Step By Step Walkthrough

Adding Additional Fields to List Page Views

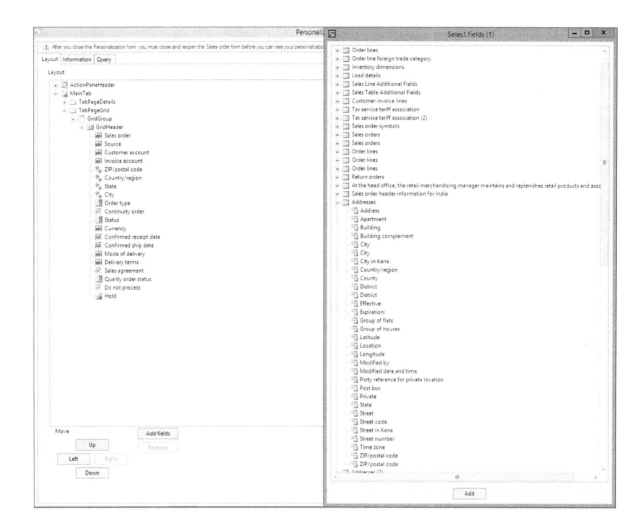

If you want to report off geographic information then you can click City, State, ZIP/Postal Code and Country/Region fields and then click on the Add button to add them to the form. When you have done selecting your additional fields then just close down the Field Explorer.

Step By Step Walkthrough

Adding Additional Fields to List Page Views

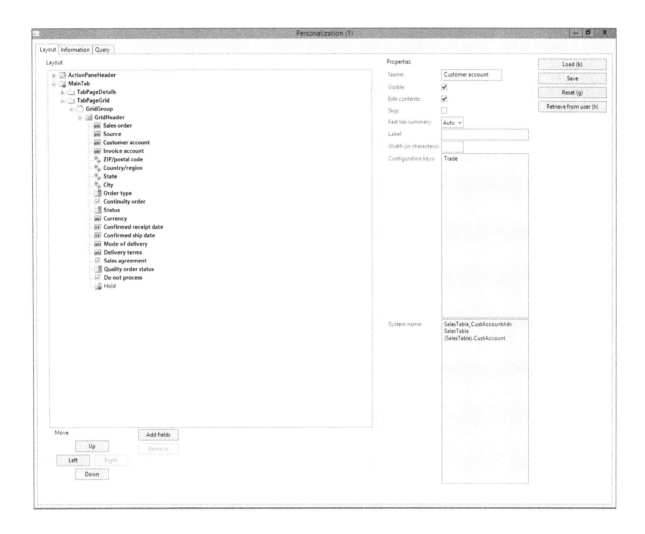

When you return to the Personalization form you see that the fields have been added with little green + signs beside them which mean that these are custom fields that have been added to the view. When you are done here you can close down the form by clicking on the Close icon in the top right hand corner of the window.

Step By Step Walkthrough

Adding Additional Fields to List Page Views

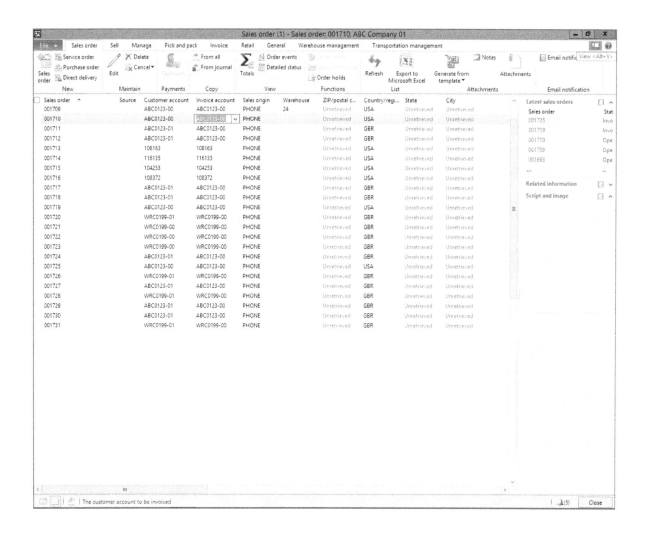

When you return back to the form you will notice that some of the fields have not been populated yet. Don't worry. All you need to do here is press F5 to refresh the view.

Step By Step Walkthrough

Adding Additional Fields to List Page Views

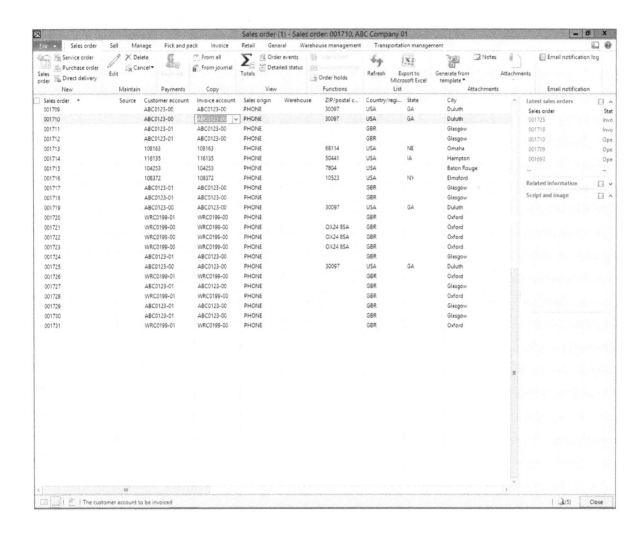

Now all of the new data will be displayed on the form for you and all of the new fields are displayed on the list page as columns that you can use for your own reporting.

Not everyone wants the same fields to show up on their forms, and no-one wants the fields that everyone else wants cluttering up their list pages that they use every dat. This is a great way to get information that you need onto your forms without having to do any development and also a very fast way to add additional information that you may only need for a little while and then remove them later on.

daxc
www.dynamicsaxcompanions.com
Dynamics AX Companions
- 27 -
www.blindsquirrelpublishing.com
© 2015 Blind Squirrel Publishing, LLC , All Rights Reserved
BLIND SQUIRREL
PUBLISHING

Filtering the Data within the List Pages

Even though the list pages are great, what users are really trying to do when they get reports is to hone in on the particular information that they are interested in. Within the list pages, the users are able to do that through the filtering options within Dynamics AX.

daxc

www.dynamicsaxcompanions.com
Dynamics AX Companions

- 29 -

www.blindsquirrelpublishing.com
© 2015 Blind Squirrel Publishing, LLC , All Rights Reserved

BLIND SQUIRREL
PUBLISHING

Step By Step Walkthrough

Filtering the Data within the List Pages

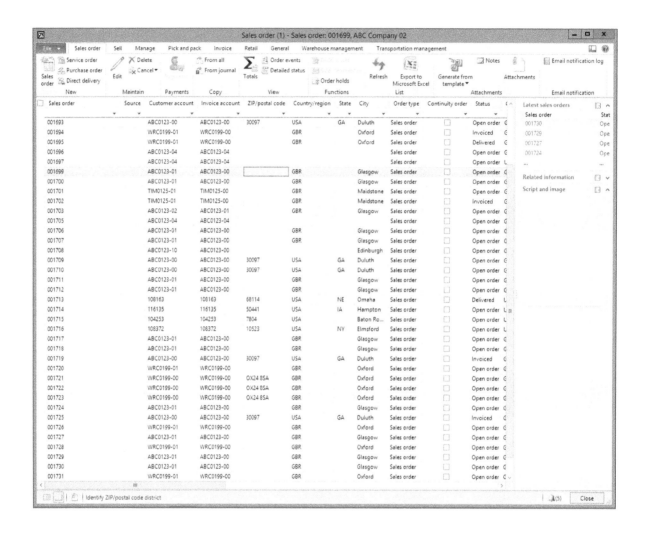

One of the best ways to filter the data is through the grid filter function. This allows the users to filter on any field that is shown within the list page. To enable this feature all you need to do is press **CTRL+G** and the search bar will show at the top of the list page.

Step By Step Walkthrough

Filtering the Data within the List Pages

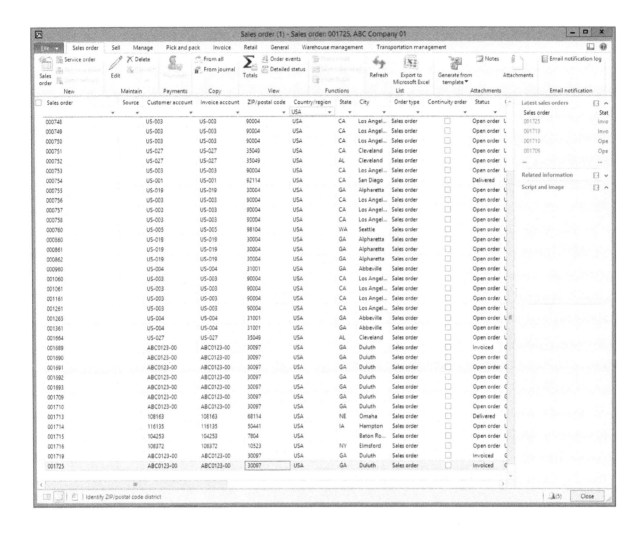

All you need to do is type in the filter query within the header row and the data will be filtered out for you. For example, in our example we just typed in **USA** into the **Country/Region** column and all the records were filtered out to the US orders.

Using the Filter by Selection within List Pages

Another way that you can quickly filter out the data that you are displaying on the list page is to use the **Filter In Grid** function which allows you to just filter out the data based on a field that you select.

Step By Step Walkthrough

Using the Filter by Selection within List Pages

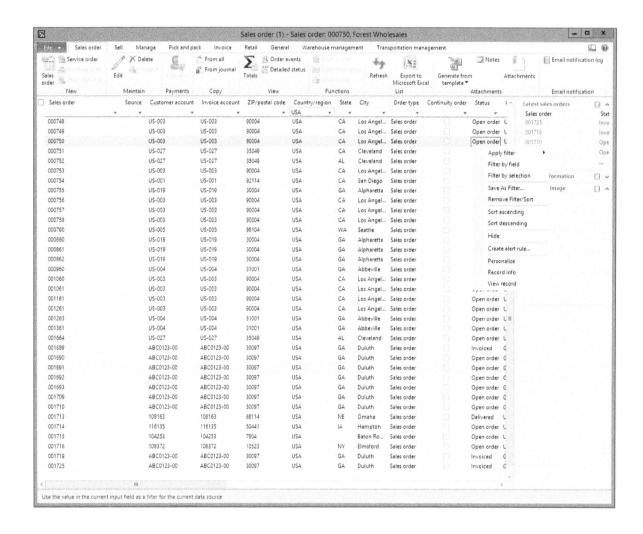

To do this, just find the field that you want to select all of the matching records for – in our case it's the **Open Order Status** on the sales orders, right-mouse-click on the it and select the **Filter By Selection** option from the context menu.

daxc   www.dynamicsaxcompanions.com
Dynamics AX Companions
- 34 -
www.blindsquirrelpublishing.com
© 2015 Blind Squirrel Publishing, LLC , All Rights Reserved

BLIND SQUIRREL
PUBLISHING

Step By Step Walkthrough

Using the Filter by Selection within List Pages

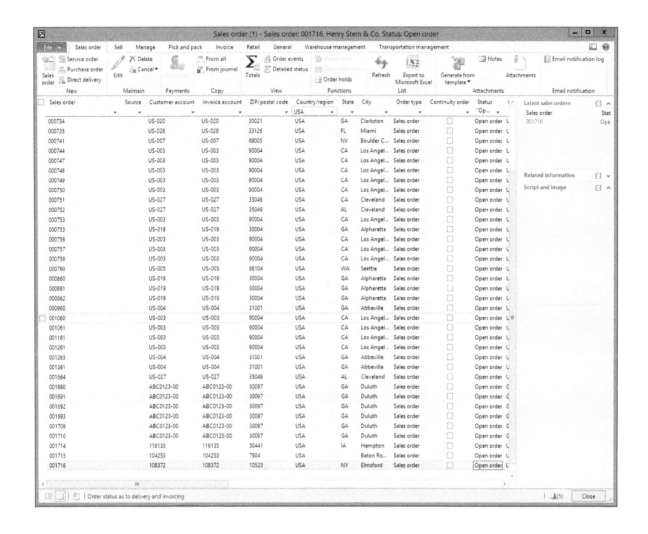

That will filter out all of the data within the grid just to the records that match.

Saving Query As A Filter

After you create a query that is useful, you may want to save it away so that you don't have to create it again and again. If you are on a form though that does not have the **Save As Query** button you have to know the trick as to where to find the option

daxc
www.dynamicsaxcompanions.com
Dynamics AX Companions

- 37 -

www.blindsquirrelpublishing.com
© 2015 Blind Squirrel Publishing, LLC , All Rights Reserved

BLIND SQUIRREL
PUBLISHING

Step By Step Walkthrough

Saving Query As A Filter

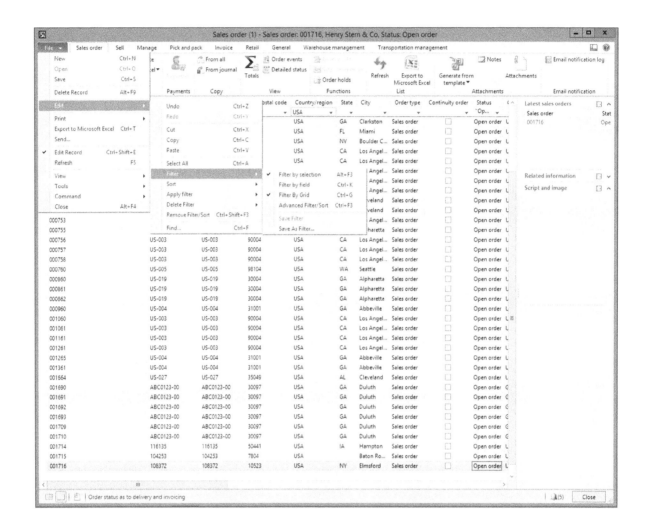

To save a query that you have just created so that you can reload it, click on the **File** menu, select the **Edit**, then **Filter** and then the **Save As Filter** menu item.

daxc www.dynamicsaxcompanions.com
Dynamics AX Companions
- 38 -
www.blindsquirrelpublishing.com
© 2015 Blind Squirrel Publishing, LLC , All Rights Reserved

BLIND SQUIRREL
PUBLISHING

Step By Step Walkthrough

Saving Query As A Filter

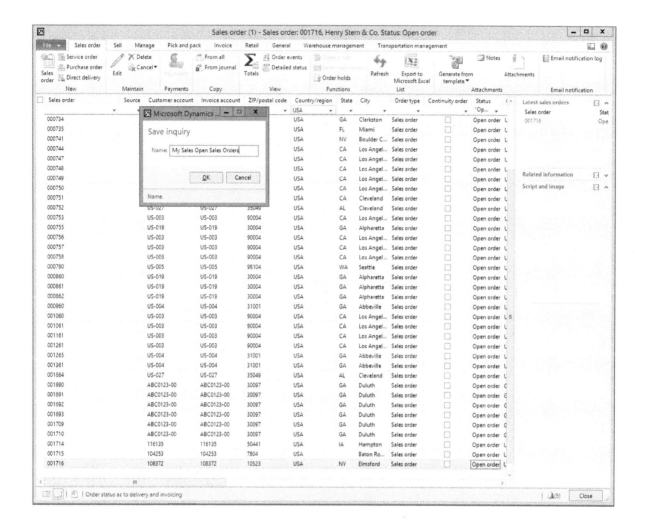

This will open up the **Save Inquiry** dialog box and you will be able to give your filter a **Name** and then click on the **OK** button.

Creating Autoreports from Data Lists

Now that we have created a list page that has just the fields that we want and also just the data that we need we can start doing more with it and start using it as the source for more ad-hoc reports. If you just want to create a simple report from the data then you can use the **Autoreport** feature and have Dynamics AX build a traditional report on the fly.

Step By Step Walkthrough

Creating Autoreports from Data Lists

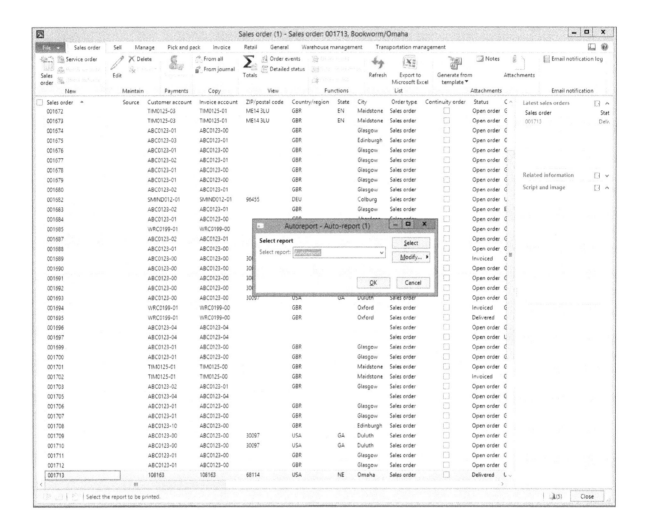

Creating Autoreports is one of the simplest things that you can do. All you need to do is press **CTRL+P** which will open up the Autoreport dialog box and you just need to click on the **OK** button.

Step By Step Walkthrough

Creating Autoreports from Data Lists

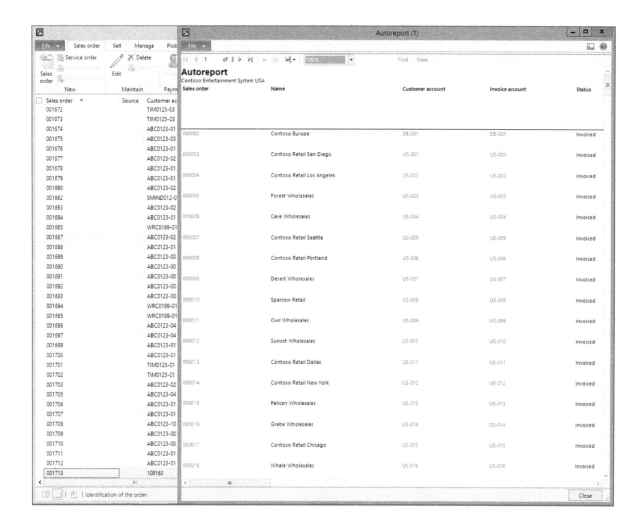

Next thing you know you will have a report with all of the data that you selected and you can save it off, e-mail it, print it, or anything else that you would want to do.

Exporting Dynamics AX List Page Data to Excel

One of the most powerful reporting features that you can take advantage of as a user is the option to export your data from any list page directly out to Excel. This is not just a screen scrape of the data though the data is linked back from Excel to Dynamics AX, making this a dynamic report that you can refresh.

daxc
www.dynamicsaxcompanions.com
Dynamics AX Companions

- 45 -

www.blindsquirrelpublishing.com
© 2015 Blind Squirrel Publishing, LLC , All Rights Reserved

BLIND SQUIRREL
PUBLISHING

Step By Step Walkthrough

Exporting Dynamics AX List Page Data to Excel

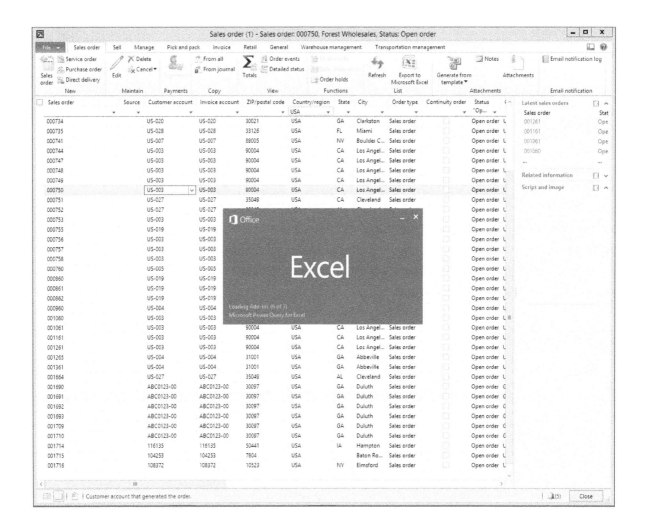

To quickly export the data out to Excel, you can usually just click on the **Export to Microsoft Excel** button that you can find on most of the forms, although you can get the data out even more quickly just by pressing **CTRL+T**.

BLIND SQUIRREL
PUBLISHING

Step By Step Walkthrough

Exporting Dynamics AX List Page Data to Excel

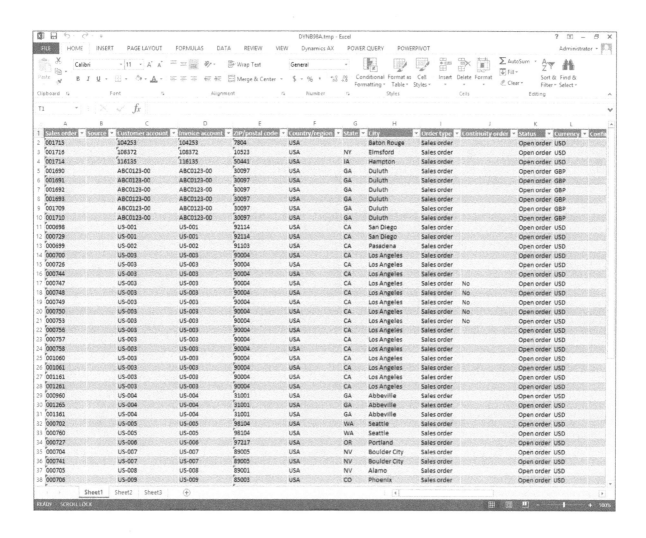

Next thing you know you will have all of the data that you had on your list page within Excel, including all of the additional fields and also any filters that you applied to the data.

www.dynamicsaxcompanions.com
Dynamics AX Companions

- 47 -

www.blindsquirrelpublishing.com
© 2015 Blind Squirrel Publishing, LLC , All Rights Reserved

BLIND SQUIRREL
PUBLISHING

Making Excel Exports Refreshable (or Static)

When you export out the data from Dynamics AX to Excel, the data can either be static, and just a copy of the data or it can be a dynamically linked back to the data within Dynamics AX and refreshable. I don't know about you all, but I prefer the second option, and here is a trick that shows you how to turn this feature on or off.

Step By Step Walkthrough

Making Excel Exports Refreshable (or Static)

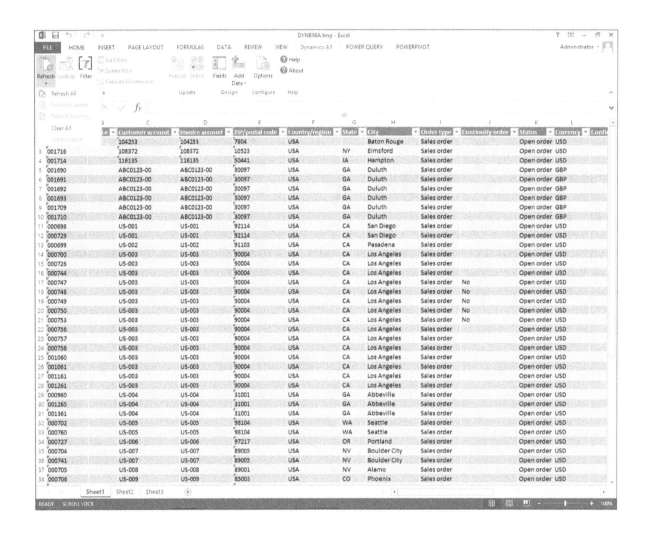

If your data is refreshable then you will notice that within the Dynamics AX tab within Excel there is a **Refresh** button that you can click on to update the data. If this option has been disabled then this button will be disabled.

Step By Step Walkthrough

Making Excel Exports Refreshable (or Static)

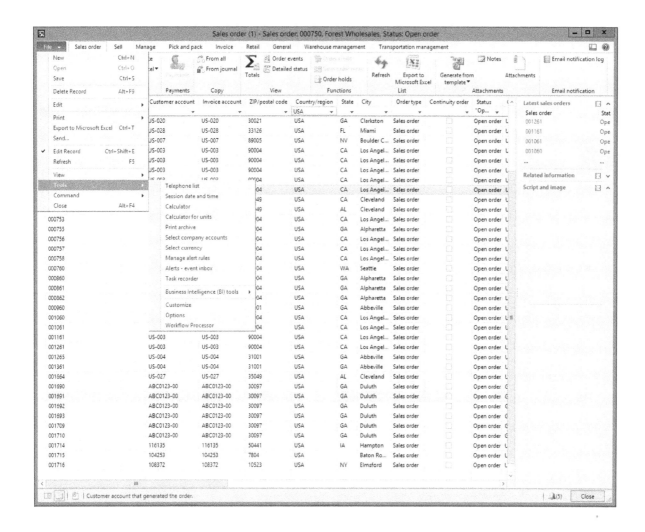

To change the export option, just click on the **File** menu within the Dynamics AX rick client, select the **Tools** sub menu and then click on the **Options** menu item.

Step By Step Walkthrough

Making Excel Exports Refreshable (or Static)

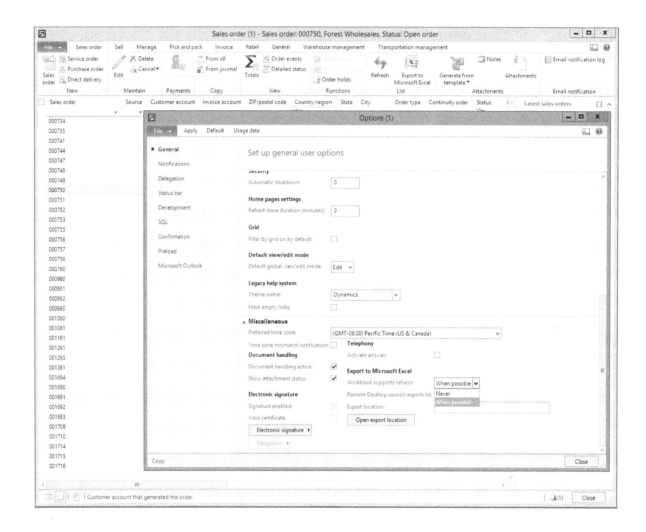

Within the **General** page of the **Options** form, scroll down to the bottom of the form and within the **Miscellaneous** field group you will see a **Workbook Supports Refresh** field. If you set this to **When Possible** then you will be able to refresh your exported data from Excel – most of the time.

Adding Additional Fields to the Excel Query

The flexibility of the Excel exports does not stop with the ability to refresh the data. The linked data is also connected with the default data sources for the form as well and as a result, you can add additional fields to the Excel worksheet that were not in the original export that you did giving you the added benefit of being able to create even better reports within Excel.

Step By Step Walkthrough

Adding Additional Fields to the Excel Query

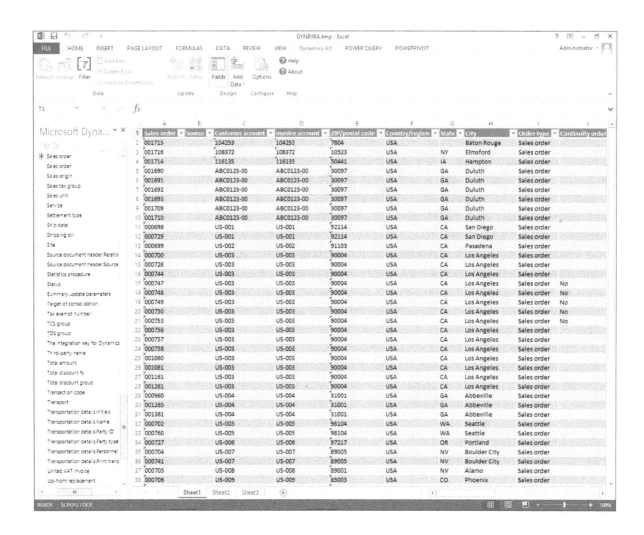

To add addition fields to the Excel Export, all you need to do is click on the **Fields** button within the **Design** group of the **Dynamics AX** ribbon bar.

Step By Step Walkthrough

Adding Additional Fields to the Excel Query

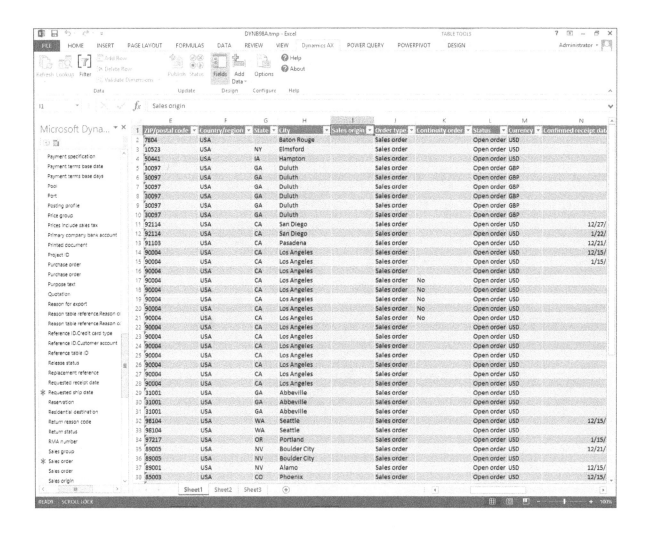

This will open up the **Dynamics AX Field Explorer** panel on the left hand side of the worksheet. All you need to do now is drag the field the you want to add to the worksheet over to the worksheet itself. If this example we added the **Sales Origin** field to the exported data.

Step By Step Walkthrough

Adding Additional Fields to the Excel Query

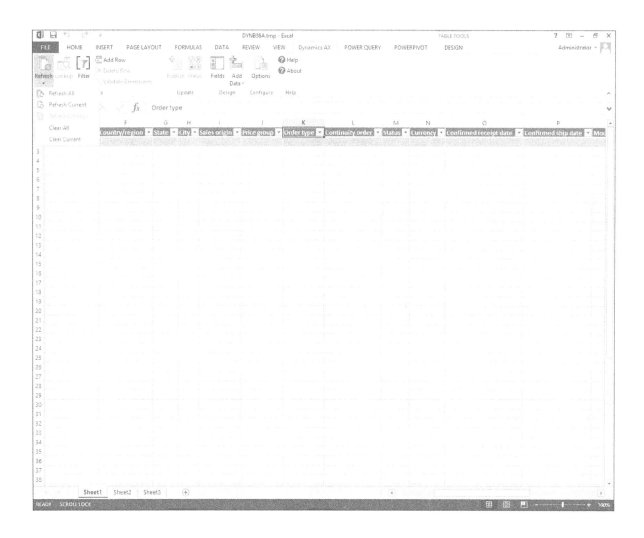

When you are done you can click on the **Fields** button again to return to the data view and then click on the **Refresh** button within the **Dynamics AX** ribbon bar.

Step By Step Walkthrough

Adding Additional Fields to the Excel Query

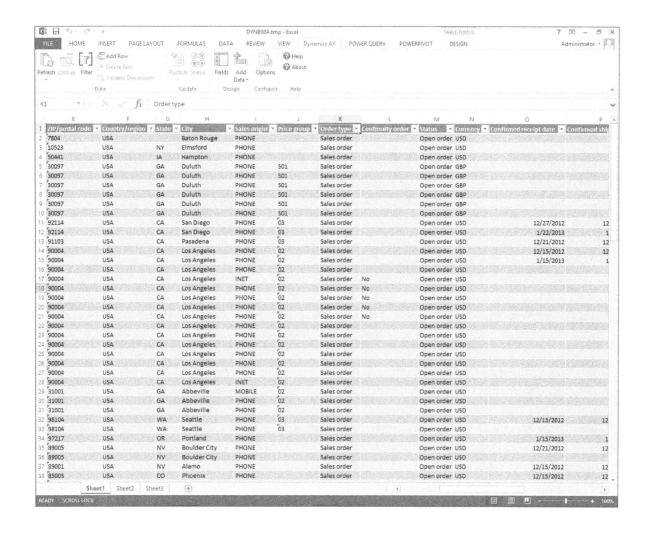

The next thing that you know you will have all of the data returned back from Dynamics AX, including the data from your new field that you just added.

Changing the Filter within the Excel Worksheet

The filters that you applied to the Dynamics AX form before being exported out to Excel are also part of the Excel worksheet query and you can tweak these within the Excel worksheet as well to create different queries and reports.

daxc   www.dynamicsaxcompanions.com
Dynamics AX Companions

- 59 -

www.blindsquirrelpublishing.com
© 2015 Blind Squirrel Publishing, LLC , All Rights Reserved

BLIND SQUIRREL
PUBLISHING

Step By Step Walkthrough

Changing the Filter within the Excel Worksheet

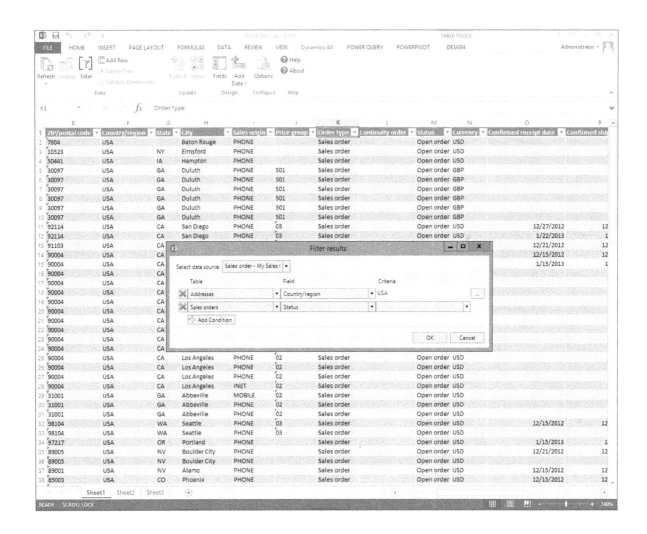

To access the filter query within Excel, just click on the **Filter** button within the **Data** group of the **Dynamics AX** ribbon bar. This will open up the **Filter Results** dialog box and you will be able to see any filters that are applied to the current query.

Step By Step Walkthrough

Changing the Filter within the Excel Worksheet

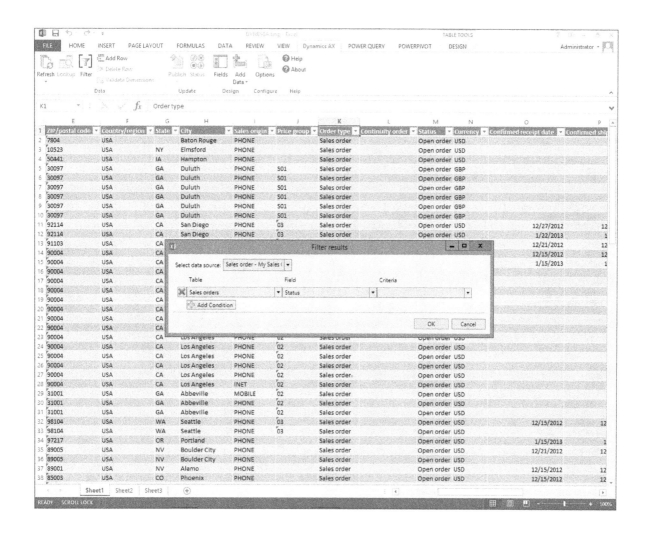

You can add or delete filters through this dialog. In this example we deleted the filter on the country so that we can get back all of the sales orders, not just the ones within the **USA** region. When you have updated your filter, just click on the **OK** button to close the form.

Step By Step Walkthrough

Changing the Filter within the Excel Worksheet

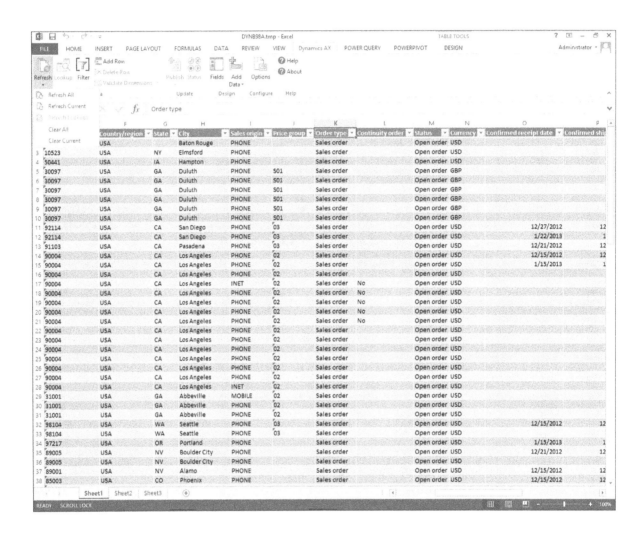

Now click on the **Refresh** button within the **Dynamics AX** ribbon bar.

Step By Step Walkthrough

Changing the Filter within the Excel Worksheet

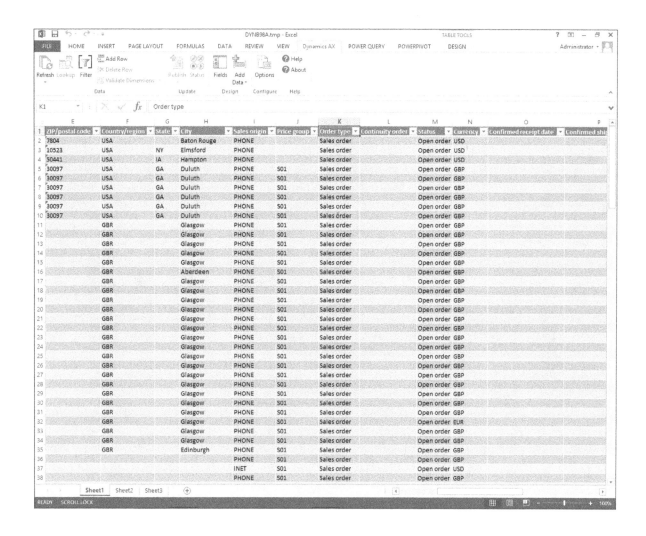

When the data refreshes you will see that you have more data returned, including orders from all of the Countries rather than just the **USA** region.

Creating Power View Dashboards within Excel

Although excel workbooks are good for viewing all of the data from Dynamics AX, we can do much better than that by turning our data into Power View dashboards

daxc
www.dynamicsaxcompanions.com
Dynamics AX Companions

- 65 -

www.blindsquirrelpublishing.com
© 2015 Blind Squirrel Publishing, LLC , All Rights Reserved

BLIND SQUIRREL
PUBLISHING

Step By Step Walkthrough

Creating Power View Dashboards within Excel

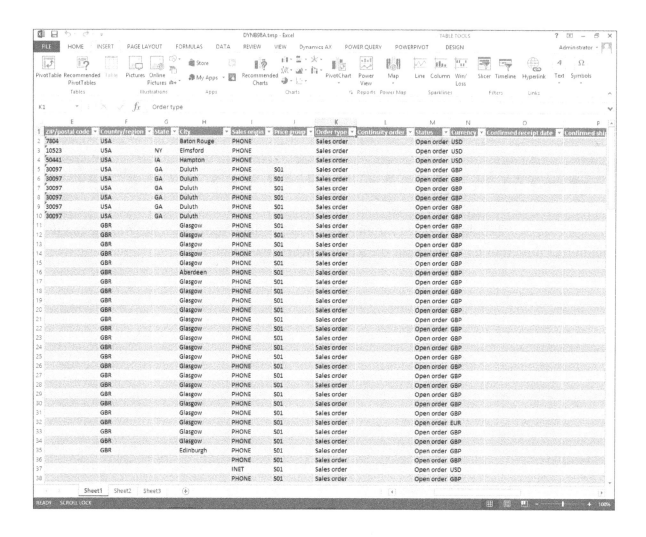

To create a **Power View** dashboard, all you need to do is click on the **Power View** button within the **Reports** group of the **INSERT** ribbon bar.

Step By Step Walkthrough

Creating Power View Dashboards within Excel

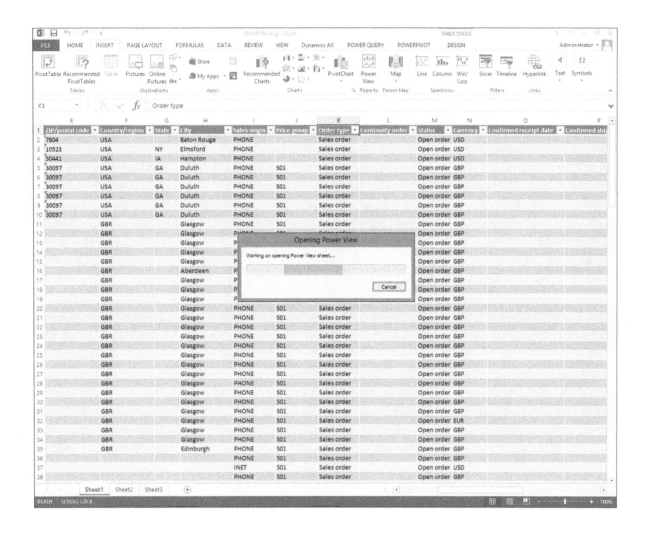

This will cause Excel to gather up all of the data that you have in the current table and make it available to **Power View**.

www.dynamicsaxcompanions.com
Dynamics AX Companions
- 67 -
www.blindsquirrelpublishing.com
© 2015 Blind Squirrel Publishing, LLC , All Rights Reserved
BLIND SQUIRREL
PUBLISHING

Step By Step Walkthrough

Creating Power View Dashboards within Excel

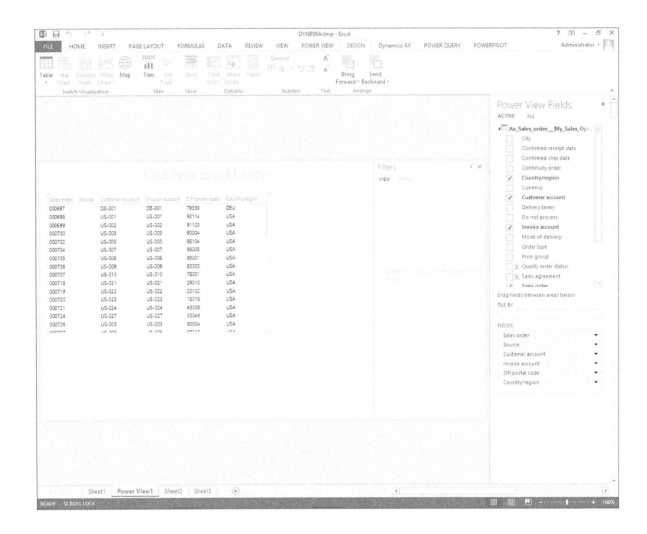

Within a few seconds you will have a new **Power View** canvas and all of the columns that were in the exported data will now be reportable **Power View Fields**. Also, **Power View** will create an initial report for you with some of the data from the report.

daxc
www.dynamicsaxcompanions.com
Dynamics AX Companions
- 68 -
www.blindsquirrelpublishing.com
© 2015 Blind Squirrel Publishing, LLC, All Rights Reserved
BLIND SQUIRREL
PUBLISHING

Step By Step Walkthrough

Creating Power View Dashboards within Excel

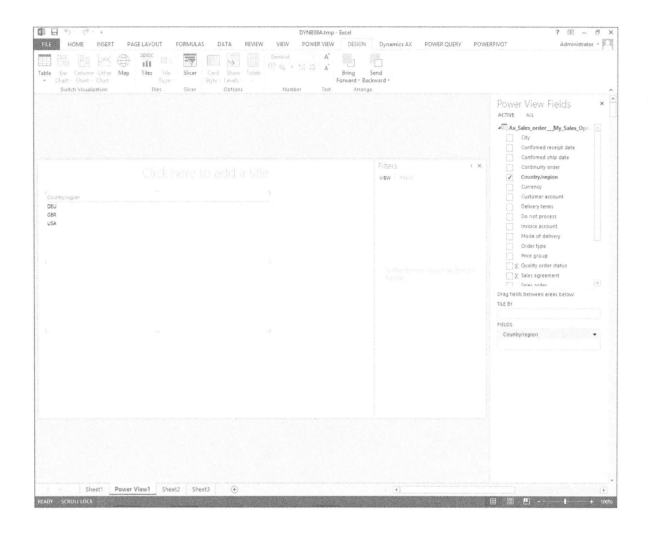

Although the initial report is good, chances are you don't really need all of the fields so you can remove all of the fields that you don't need from the **Fields** list within the right hand panel. Here we took out all of the fields except for the **Country/Region**.

daxc
www.dynamicsaxcompanions.com
Dynamics AX Companions

- 69 -

www.blindsquirrelpublishing.com
© 2015 Blind Squirrel Publishing, LLC , All Rights Reserved

BLIND SQUIRREL
PUBLISHING

Step By Step Walkthrough

Creating Power View Dashboards within Excel

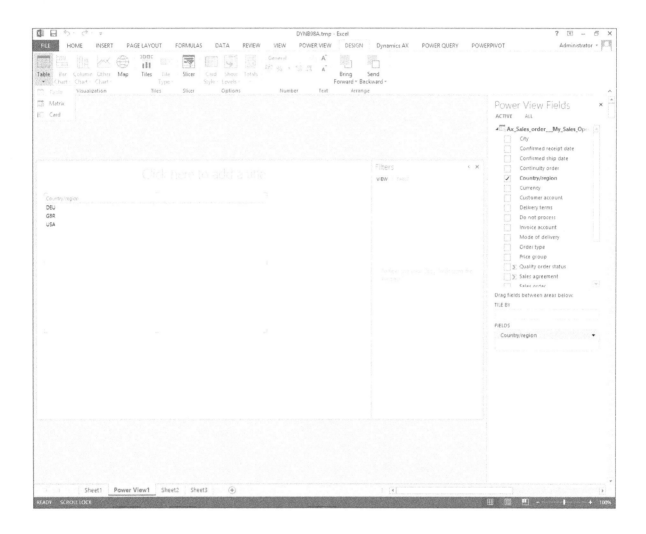

The report that is created by default is also just a table style report. To make this report a little more flexible, click on the **Table** button and change the table type to **Matrix**.

Step By Step Walkthrough

Creating Power View Dashboards within Excel

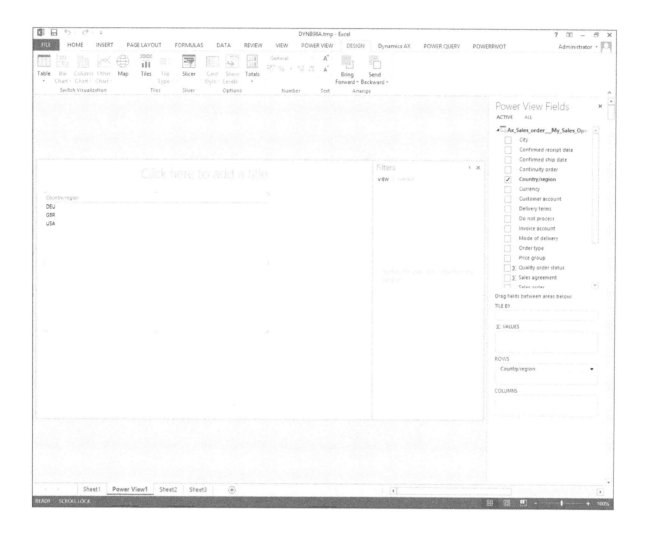

If you look at the Power View panel to the right of the canvas you will notice that the field options have changed a little to allow you to have Rows and Columns within your report.

da★c   www.dynamicsaxcompanions.com
Dynamics AX Companions
- 71 -
www.blindsquirrelpublishing.com
© 2015 Blind Squirrel Publishing, LLC , All Rights Reserved

BLIND SQUIRREL
PUBLISHING

Step By Step Walkthrough

Creating Power View Dashboards within Excel

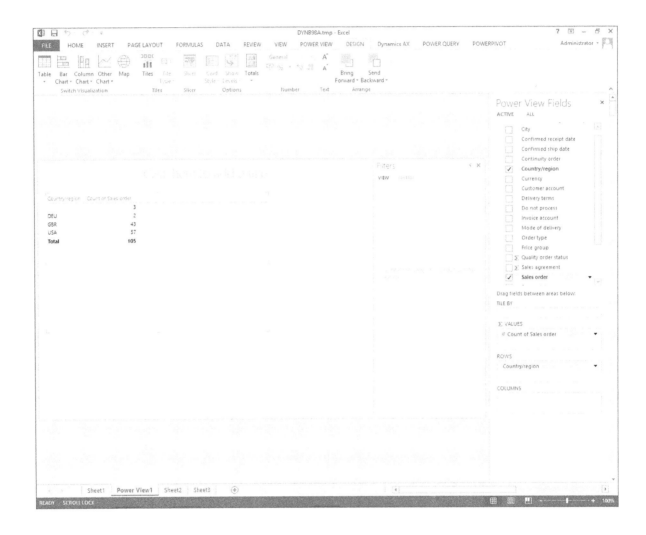

To start creating some data for this report we need to add a **Measure** to the report. So in this example we just drag the **Sales Order** field to the **VALUES** field. This automatically sums up the number of records showing us the total number of sales orders by region.

Viewing the Query within PowerPivot

When we told Excel to create a Power View report from our data it did something behind the scenes that now we can take advantage of. It took the data and added it as a **Power Pivot** data set. This is very useful because this allows us to tweak the data even more.

daxc
www.dynamicsaxcompanions.com
Dynamics AX Companions

- 73 -

www.blindsquirrelpublishing.com
© 2015 Blind Squirrel Publishing, LLC , All Rights Reserved

BLIND SQUIRREL
PUBLISHING

Step By Step Walkthrough

Viewing the Query within PowerPivot

To view the data within **Power Pivot** all you need to do is click on the **Manage** button within the **Data Model** group of the **Power Pivot** ribbon bar.

www.dynamicsaxcompanions.com
Dynamics AX Companions

- 74 -

www.blindsquirrelpublishing.com
© 2015 Blind Squirrel Publishing, LLC , All Rights Reserved

BLIND SQUIRREL
PUBLISHING

Step By Step Walkthrough

Viewing the Query within PowerPivot

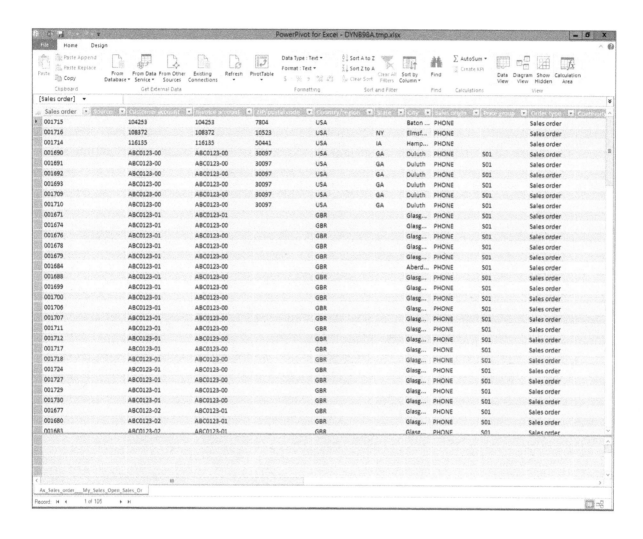

This will open up the **Power Pivot** workspace and you will be able to see all of the data that we loaded in and also all of the different manipulation options that we have for this data.

da×c www.dynamicsaxcompanions.com
Dynamics AX Companions
- 75 -
www.blindsquirrelpublishing.com
© 2015 Blind Squirrel Publishing, LLC , All Rights Reserved
BLIND SQUIRREL
PUBLISHING

Adding New Columns to Power Pivot Data Models

One of the things that you always want to do with data is create more of it, usually as calculated fields or fields that are composed of other fields. You can do this within the workbook itself, but if you really want to add some pizazz to your reports and make them a little more flexible you can do it within Power Pivot.

Step By Step Walkthrough

Adding New Columns to Power Pivot Data Models

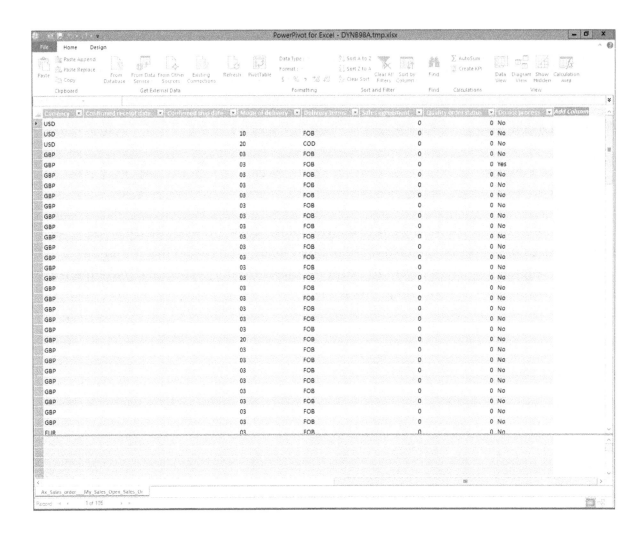

If you scroll to the right of the **Power Pivot** data model worksheet you will notice that there is a column waiting for you to add a new column.

Step By Step Walkthrough

Adding New Columns to Power Pivot Data Models

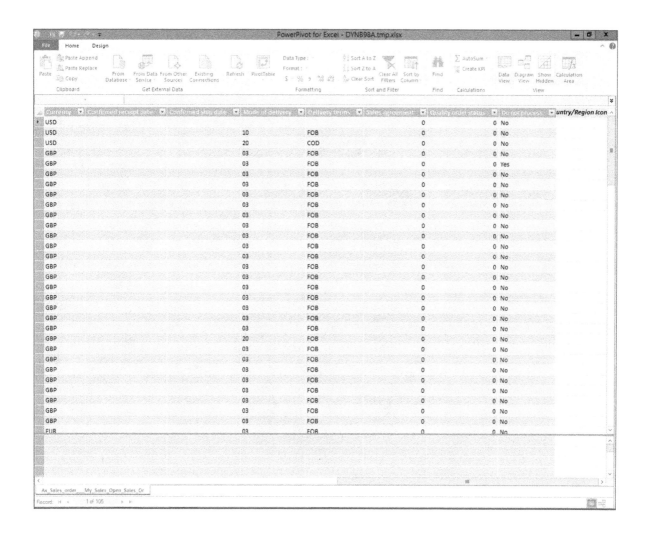

To create a new **Column** just type in the new column name. In this example we will add a new column called **Country/Region Icon**.

Step By Step Walkthrough

Adding New Columns to Power Pivot Data Models

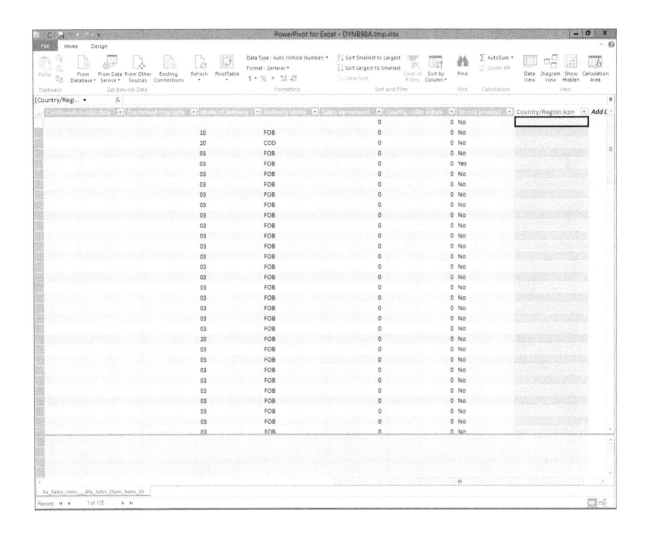

After you have named the column you will see that there is no data in it yet.

Step By Step Walkthrough

Adding New Columns to Power Pivot Data Models

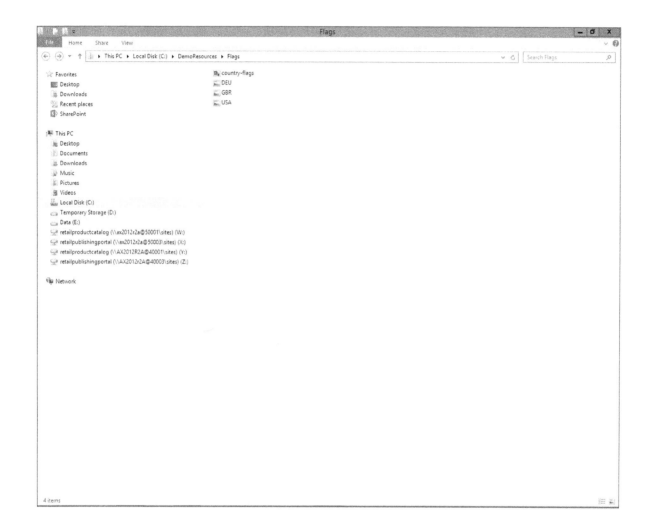

For this example we are going to create a new column that is really an image for the country that we are reporting the sales on. To prepare for this we have a folder that has all of the country flags in it with the file name being the same as the **Country/Region** field.

Step By Step Walkthrough

Adding New Columns to Power Pivot Data Models

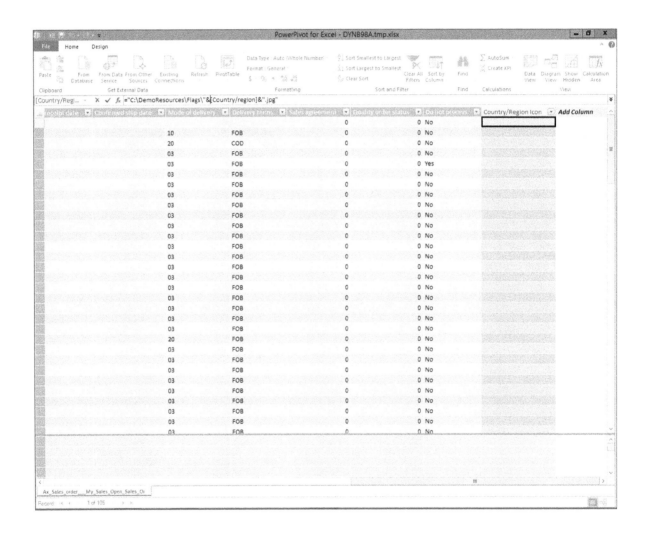

So, returning back to **Power Pivot** all we do is build a field that is a string concatenation of the **Country/Region** field and the path for the image file.

 www.dynamicsaxcompanions.com
Dynamics AX Companions

- 82 -

www.blindsquirrelpublishing.com
© 2015 Blind Squirrel Publishing, LLC , All Rights Reserved
 BLIND SQUIRREL
PUBLISHING

Step By Step Walkthrough

Adding New Columns to Power Pivot Data Models

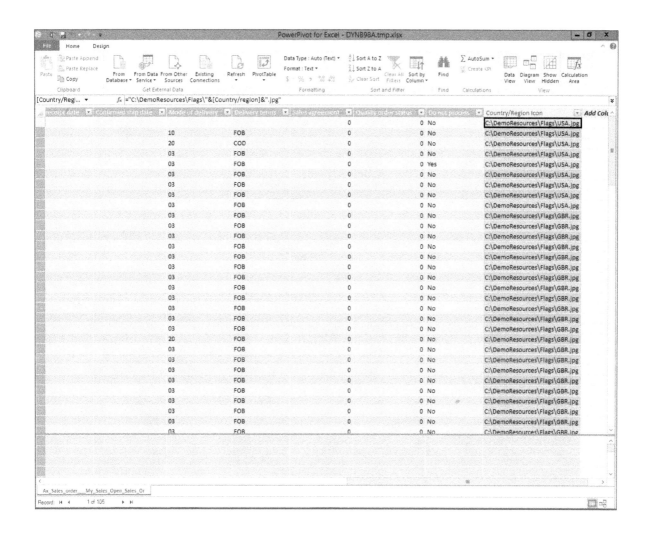

As soon as we update the formula you will see that all of the rows in the data now have a path to their respective image.

Switching To Advanced Mode within Power Pivot

Before we move to the next step we will just point out an option that we will need to enable. By default Power Pivot is in the simple mode, but for the next step we need to switch it to **Advanced** mode. If you don't do this the next step will not be possible and it will save you hours of cursing this tutorial because you can't find the options that we are going to show.

daxc
www.dynamicsaxcompanions.com
Dynamics AX Companions

- 85 -

www.blindsquirrelpublishing.com
© 2015 Blind Squirrel Publishing, LLC , All Rights Reserved

BLIND SQUIRREL
PUBLISHING

Step By Step Walkthrough

Switching To Advanced Mode within Power Pivot

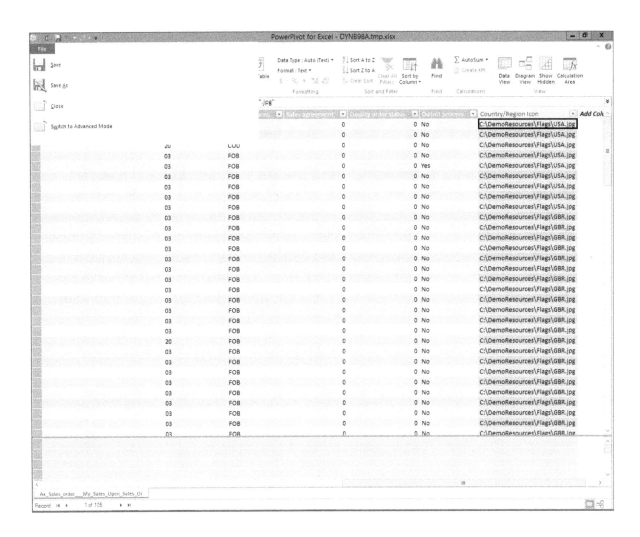

To enable the **Advanced Mode**, click on the **File** menu and select the **Switch to Advanced Mode** option.

Step By Step Walkthrough

Switching To Advanced Mode within Power Pivot

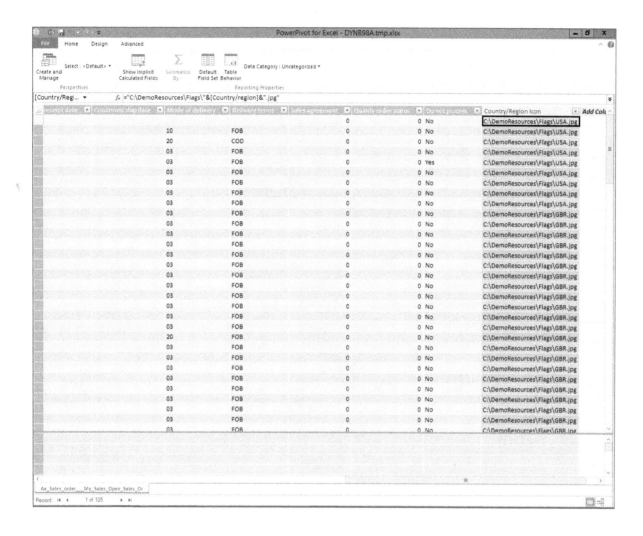

What you will notice is that there is now an **Advanced** tab within the ribbon bar.

Configuring Fields to Show as Images in Dashboards

Now that we have a field that is a file path to our country image icons we need to configure them to display within **Power View** as images.

daxc
www.dynamicsaxcompanions.com
Dynamics AX Companions

- 89 -

www.blindsquirrelpublishing.com
© 2015 Blind Squirrel Publishing, LLC , All Rights Reserved

BLIND SQUIRREL
PUBLISHING

Step By Step Walkthrough

Configuring Fields to Show as Images in Dashboards

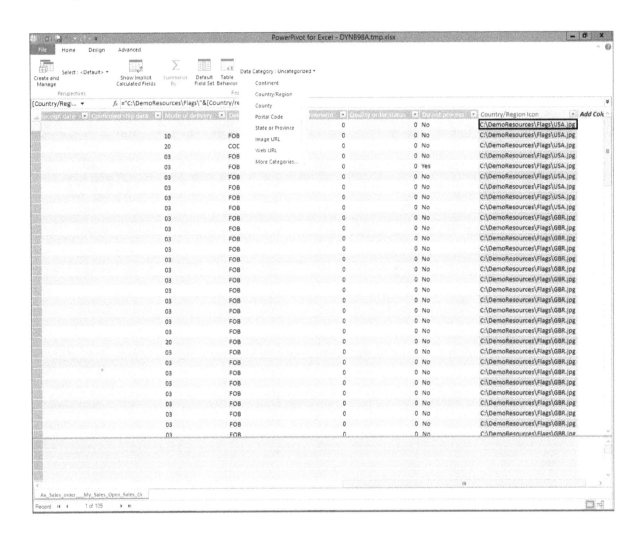

To make a field show up as an image, just select the column (**Country/Region Icon** in our case) and then within the **Advanced** ribbon bar click on the **Data Category** dropdown list and select the **Image URL** option.

Step By Step Walkthrough

Configuring Fields to Show as Images in Dashboards

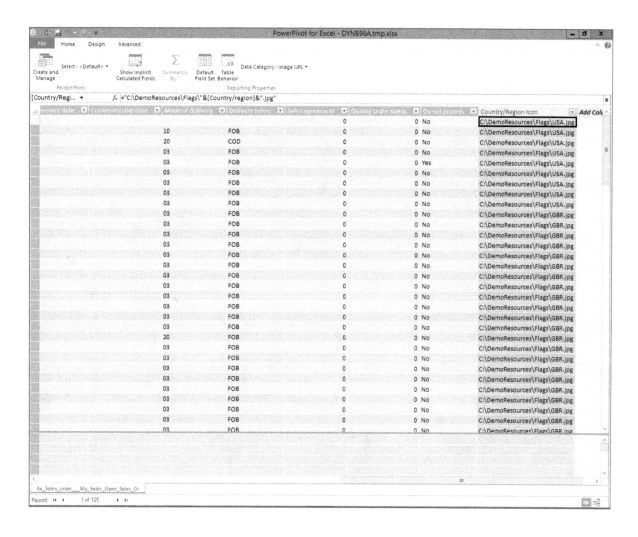

Now that you have done that, just click on the **Save** icon and then exit out of **Power Pivot**.

daxc
www.dynamicsaxcompanions.com
Dynamics AX Companions
- 91 -
www.blindsquirrelpublishing.com
© 2015 Blind Squirrel Publishing, LLC , All Rights Reserved
BLIND SQUIRREL
PUBLISHING

Step By Step Walkthrough

Configuring Fields to Show as Images in Dashboards

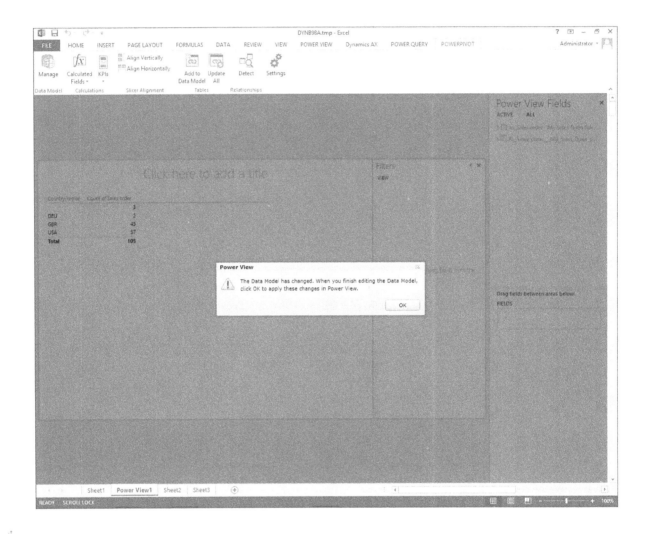

When you return back to your Excel workbook you will be told that the data model has been updated and that there are new fields available – which is right because we just added a new calculated field for the icon.

Using Images within Power View Dashboards

Now that we have an image field added to our data model we can start using it within our dashboards and really start cooking with oil.

Step By Step Walkthrough

Using Images within Power View Dashboards

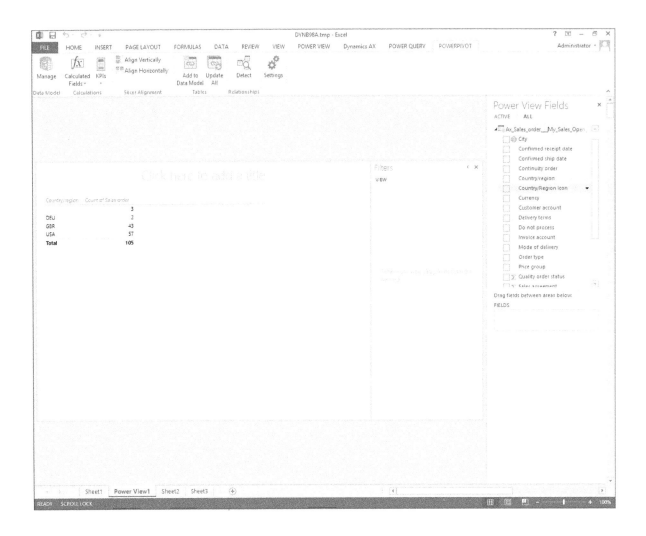

To do this, return to the **Power View** dashboard canvas and within the field list you will see that the new **Country/Region Icon** is available for you to add to the report.

daxc
www.dynamicsaxcompanions.com
Dynamics AX Companions
- 94 -
www.blindsquirrelpublishing.com
© 2015 Blind Squirrel Publishing, LLC , All Rights Reserved
BLIND SQUIRREL
PUBLISHING

Step By Step Walkthrough

Using Images within Power View Dashboards

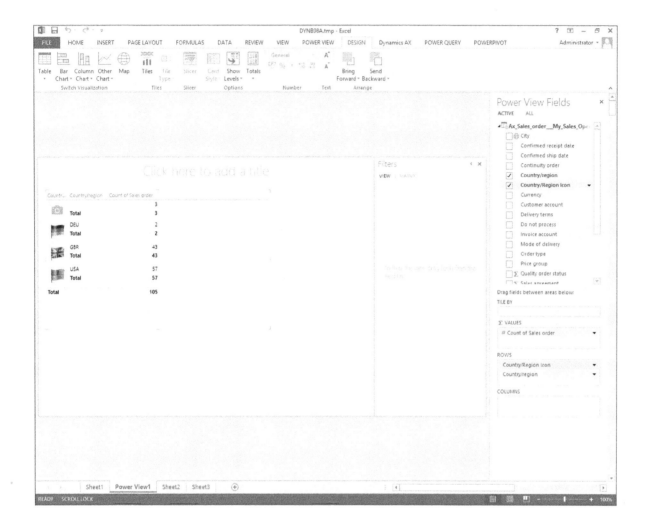

As soon as you add it to the dashboard you will see it show up as an image

Step By Step Walkthrough

Using Images within Power View Dashboards

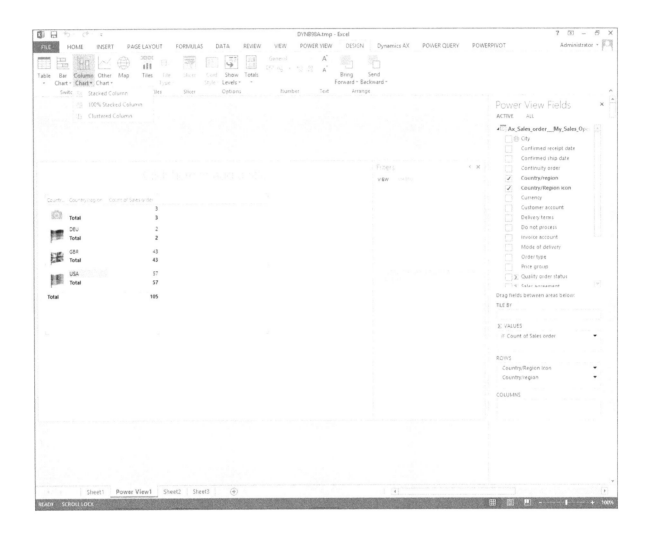

To make this chart prettier, click on the **Column Chart** button within the ribbon bar and select the **Stacked Column** option.

Step By Step Walkthrough

Using Images within Power View Dashboards

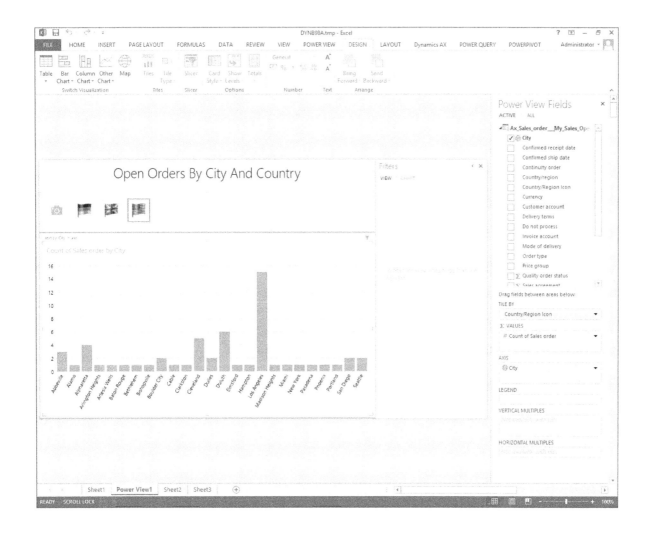

Then move the **Country/Region Icon** to the **TILE BY** field within the formatting panel to the right. This will allow you to see the data by Country and change the view by clicking on the icon.

Step By Step Walkthrough

Using Images within Power View Dashboards

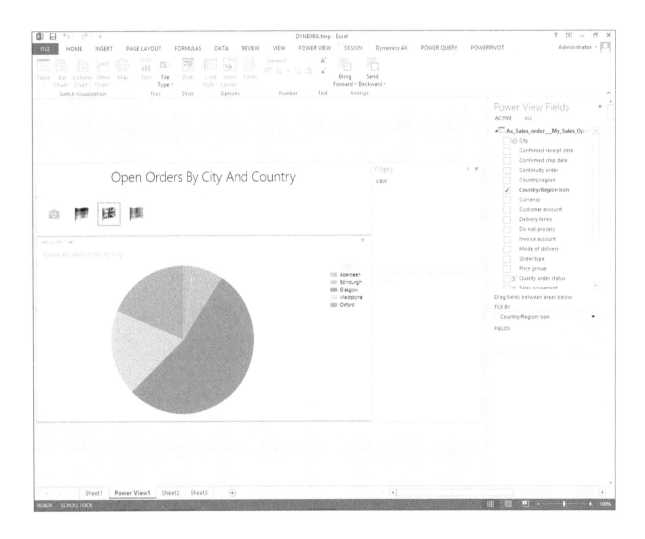

If you want to get really clever you can change more of the visualizations, and also add a Title to the dashboard. Now you have your very own dashboard report.

Creating Dashboards Directly from Dynamics AX

Excel is not the only reporting tool that users can take advantage of to create their own dashboards and reports. Power View is embedded directly within a lot of the master forms as an Analysis button that allows you to create your own dashboards and also share them with others within the organization.

daxc
www.dynamicsaxcompanions.com
Dynamics AX Companions

- 99 -

www.blindsquirrelpublishing.com
© 2015 Blind Squirrel Publishing, LLC , All Rights Reserved

BLIND SQUIRREL
PUBLISHING

Step By Step Walkthrough

Creating Dashboards Directly from Dynamics AX

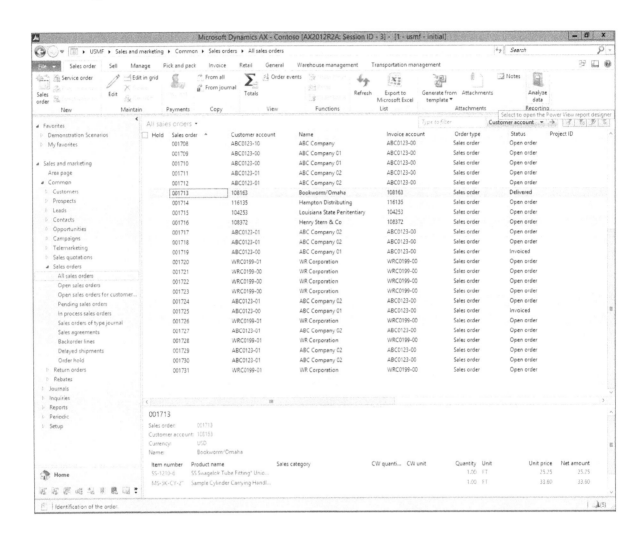

For example, if you look at the **All Sales Orders** list page, then you will see that there is an **Analyze Data** button within the **Sales Order** ribbon bar. To start creating a dashboard, all you need to do is click on it.

Step By Step Walkthrough

Creating Dashboards Directly from Dynamics AX

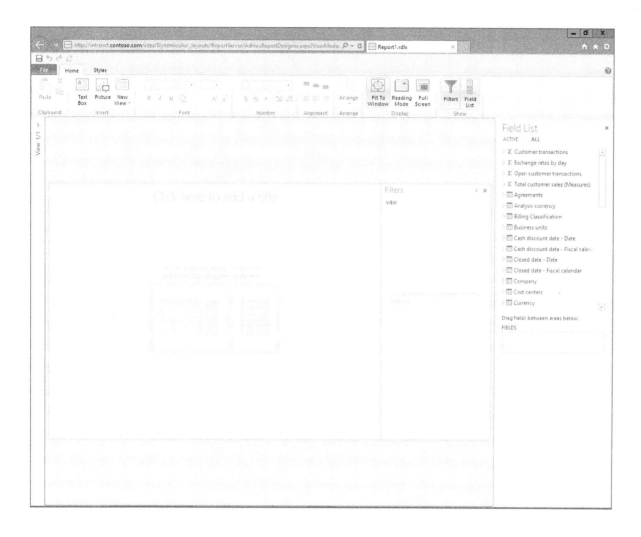

That will open up a new **Power View** canvas for you using the web interface and it will be linked with the standard **Accounts Receivable** cube that is delivered with Dynamics AX 2012.

daxc   www.dynamicsaxcompanions.com
Dynamics AX Companions
- 101 -
www.blindsquirrelpublishing.com
© 2015 Blind Squirrel Publishing, LLC , All Rights Reserved
BLIND SQUIRREL
PUBLISHING

Step By Step Walkthrough

Creating Dashboards Directly from Dynamics AX

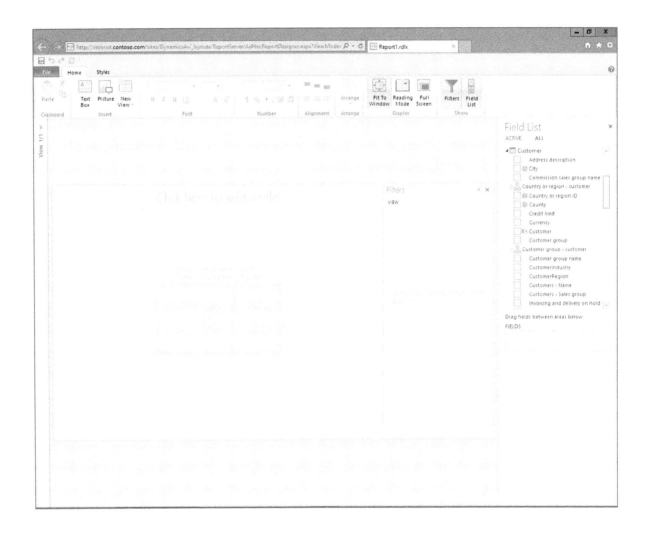

If you scroll down the **Field List** you will see that there are a lot of dimensions that you can report off right away. For example, if you expand the **Customers** field group then you will see all of the different ways that you can slice and dice the customer information.

Step By Step Walkthrough

Creating Dashboards Directly from Dynamics AX

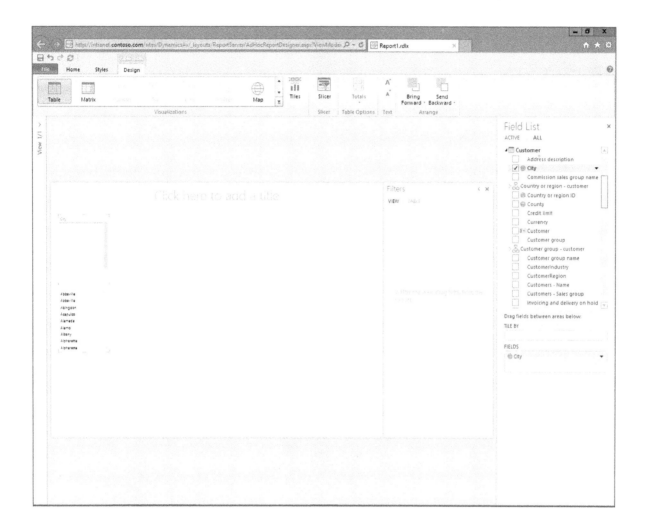

Start off by selecting the **City** dimension. This will create a new panel on the canvas and list out all of the **Cities** that are within the cube.

daxc
www.dynamicsaxcompanions.com
Dynamics AX Companions

- 103 -

www.blindsquirrelpublishing.com
© 2015 Blind Squirrel Publishing, LLC, All Rights Reserved

BLIND SQUIRREL
PUBLISHING

Step By Step Walkthrough

Creating Dashboards Directly from Dynamics AX

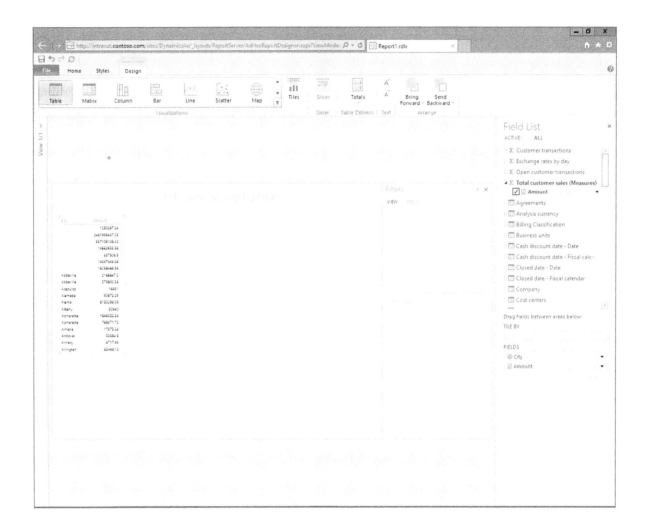

Next we need to add a measure to the chart so that we can get some values in our report. Scroll up to the top of the form, expand out the **Total Customer Sales (Measure)** group and select the **Amount** measure so that we can see the sales amount by city.

Step By Step Walkthrough

Creating Dashboards Directly from Dynamics AX

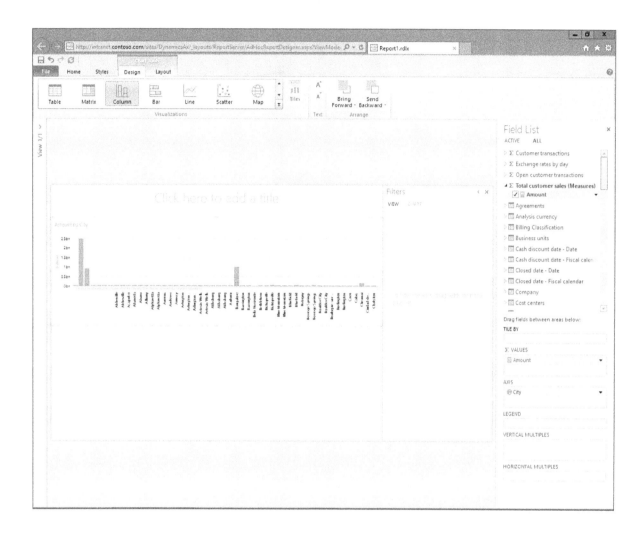

Now click on the **Column** visualization option to convert the table into a column chart.

Step By Step Walkthrough

Creating Dashboards Directly from Dynamics AX

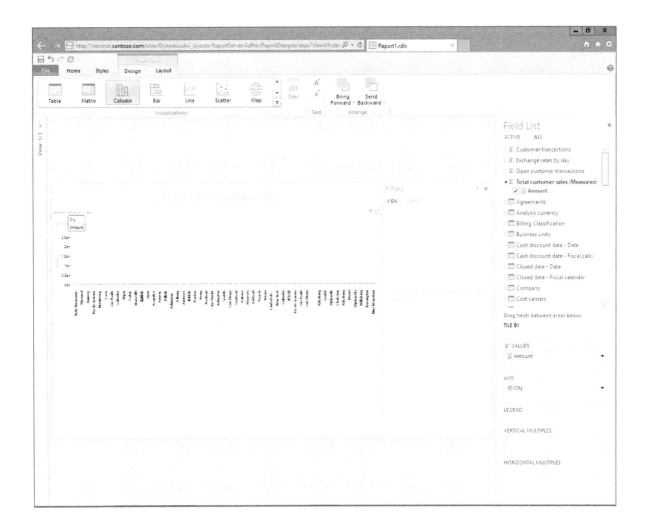

The data is not really sorted the right way, we would rather have it sorted by the amount rather than the city name, so on the chart, click on the dropdown list beside the **Sort By** field and select the **Amount** field.

Step By Step Walkthrough

Creating Dashboards Directly from Dynamics AX

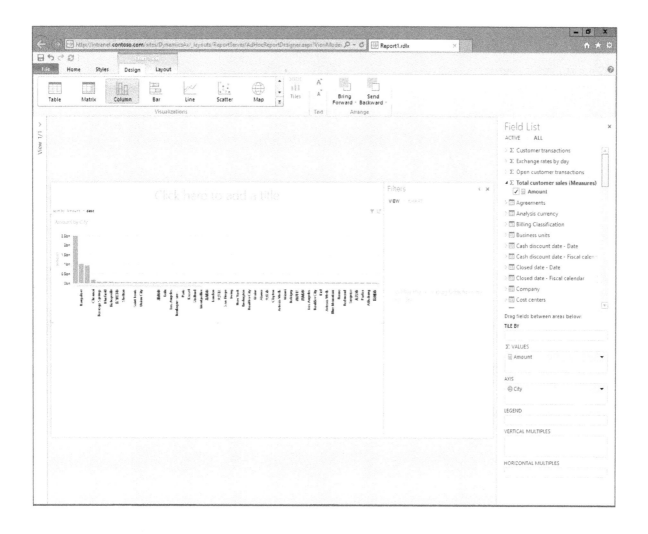

Then click on the **Asc** (Ascending) field to change the sort order to **Desc** (Descending) option. Now we see the top sales amount by city in descending order.

Step By Step Walkthrough

Creating Dashboards Directly from Dynamics AX

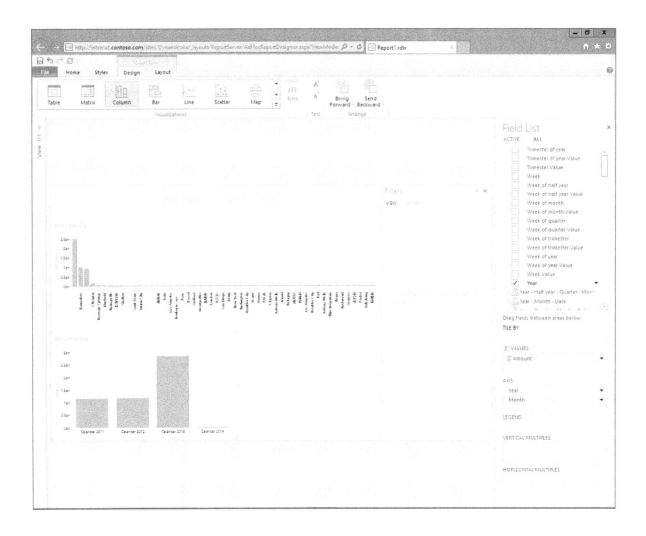

Click on a blank area of the canvas to deselect the chart that we just created and then select the **Year**, **Month**, and **Amount** dimensions and measures then convert that to a column chart as well so that we have another chart that is showing us the sales by year with a drill through into the months.

Step By Step Walkthrough

Creating Dashboards Directly from Dynamics AX

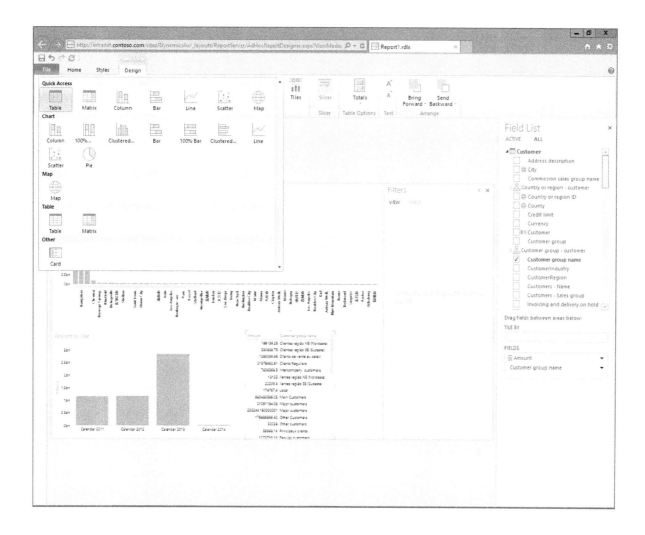

Click on a blank area of the canvas to deselect the second chart and create one more chart that has the **Amount**, and **Customer Group Name**. Now expand out the **Visualizations** and you will see that there are a few more options available to you, including a **Pie Chart.**

daxc
www.dynamicsaxcompanions.com
Dynamics AX Companions
- 109 -
www.blindsquirrelpublishing.com
© 2015 Blind Squirrel Publishing, LLC , All Rights Reserved
BLIND SQUIRREL
PUBLISHING

Step By Step Walkthrough

Creating Dashboards Directly from Dynamics AX

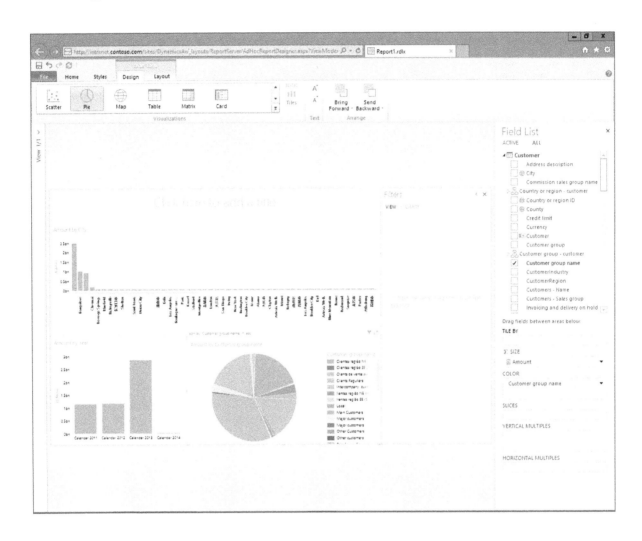

Now you can rearrange the panels so that they look nice and fit all of the information that you need to see.

Step By Step Walkthrough

Creating Dashboards Directly from Dynamics AX

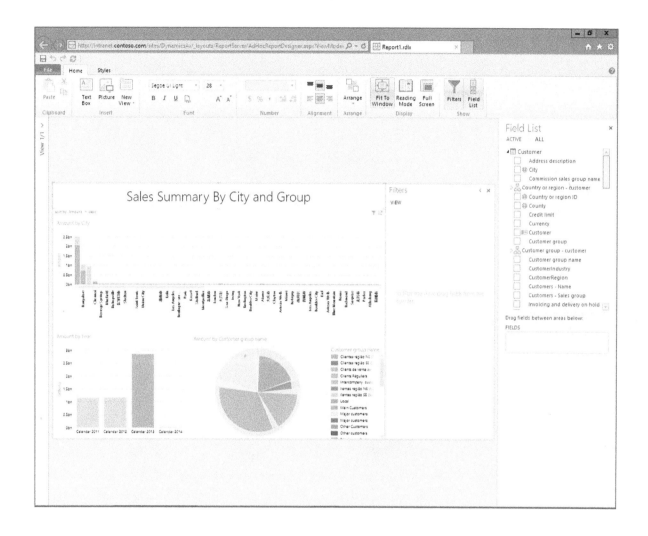

After adding a title to the chart I think we are done. You can test drive the data just by clicking on one of the annual columns and you will notice that all of the other charts get filtered out.

daxc

www.dynamicsaxcompanions.com
Dynamics AX Companions

- 111 -

www.blindsquirrelpublishing.com
© 2015 Blind Squirrel Publishing, LLC , All Rights Reserved

BLIND SQUIRREL
PUBLISHING

Saving Power View Reports to SharePoint

The web based Power View reports are a little more flexible than the reports that we created in Excel, because we can save them away to the SharePoint reporting repository and everyone is able to access the report.

Step By Step Walkthrough

Saving Power View Reports to SharePoint

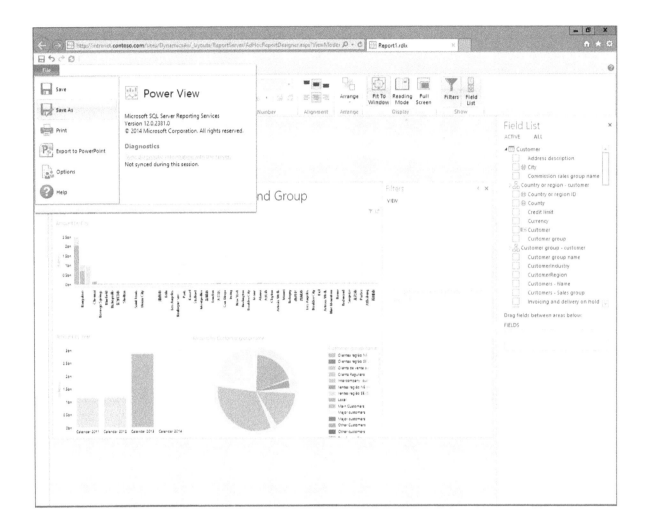

So save the reports that you create, just click on the **File** menu within the Power View designer and then select the **Save As** option.

Step By Step Walkthrough

Saving Power View Reports to SharePoint

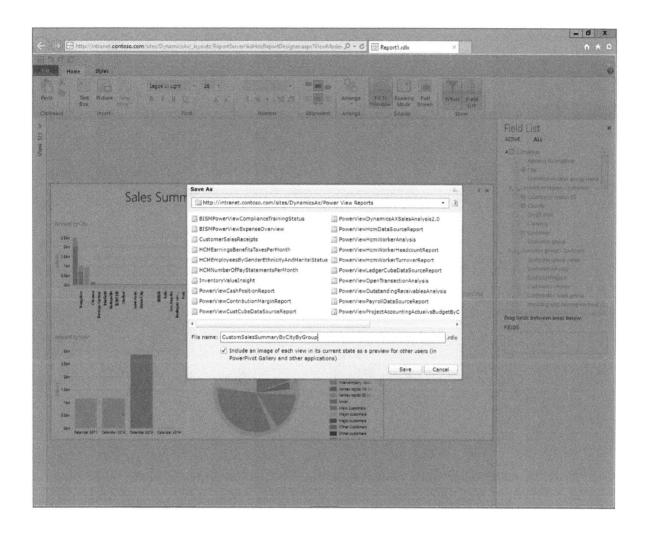

This will pop up a **Save As** dialog box and you will see all of the other reports that are already stored away for you. Just give your sashboard a new name and then click on the **Save** button.

daxc

www.dynamicsaxcompanions.com
Dynamics AX Companions

- 115 -

www.blindsquirrelpublishing.com
© 2015 Blind Squirrel Publishing, LLC , All Rights Reserved

BLIND SQUIRREL
PUBLISHING

Step By Step Walkthrough

Saving Power View Reports to SharePoint

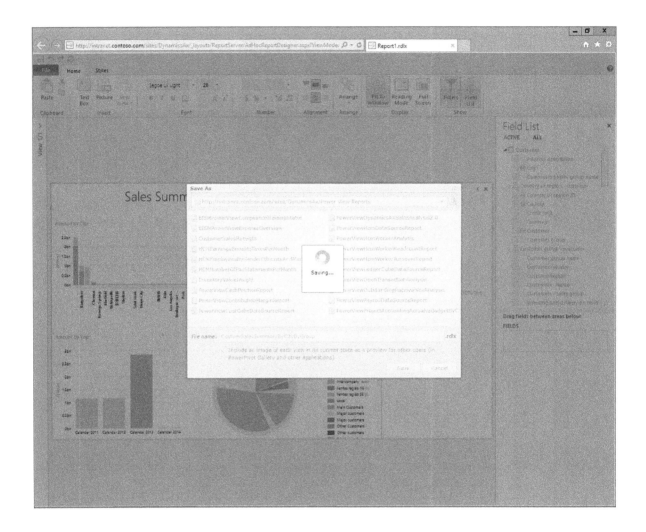

Power View will then process for a couple of seconds and save the report away into the common repositioy.

Exporting Power View Dashboards To PowerPoint

Once the report is saved to the report library you can do something that is pretty darn cool, and that is to export the dashboard out as a PowerPoint presentation. This may seem pretty straight forward because everyone is able to do a screen capture and then put it into a presentation, but wait up a little, because this does a little more than that.

Step By Step Walkthrough

Exporting Power View Dashboards To PowerPoint

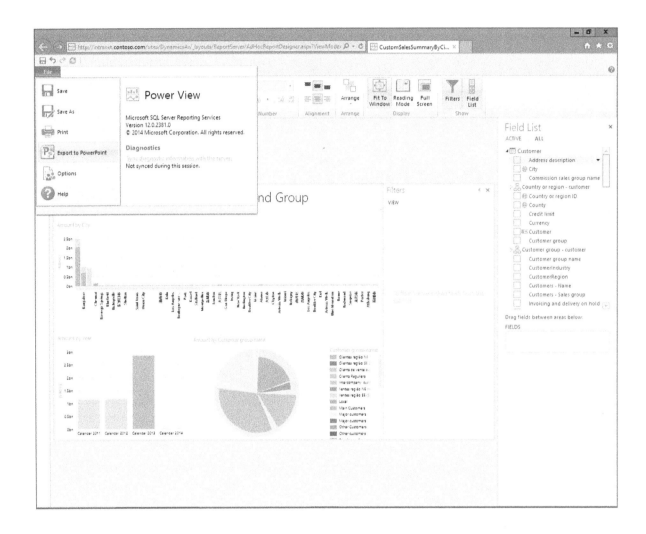

To start off, click on the **File** menu within the Power View designer and then select the **Export to PowerPoint** option.

Step By Step Walkthrough

Exporting Power View Dashboards To PowerPoint

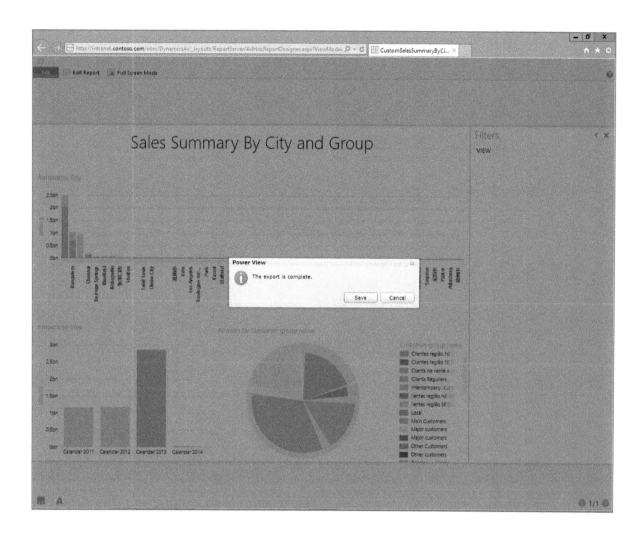

Power View will process the report for you and then ask you if you want to save it as a PowerPoint. Click on the **Save** button.

Step By Step Walkthrough

Exporting Power View Dashboards To PowerPoint

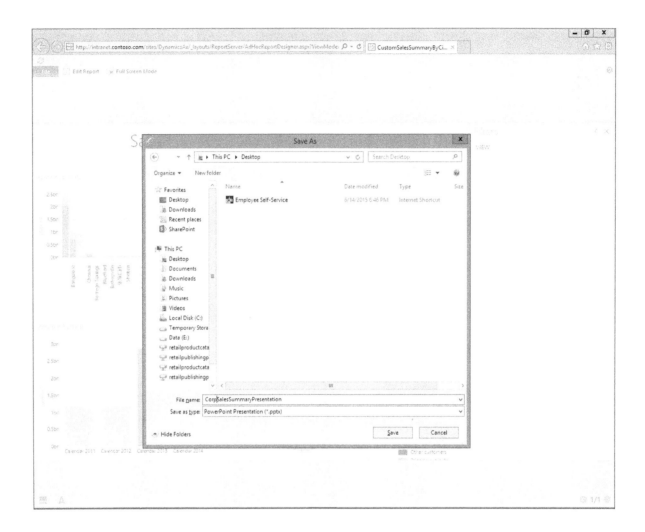

This will open up a file explorer and you can select where you want to save the PowerPoint to and you can also give your PowerPoint a name before clicking on the **Save** button.

Step By Step Walkthrough

Exporting Power View Dashboards To PowerPoint

After this is done, you can go to where you saved the PowerPoint (in this case my desktop) and then open up the file.

daxc

www.dynamicsaxcompanions.com
Dynamics AX Companions

- 121 -

www.blindsquirrelpublishing.com
© 2015 Blind Squirrel Publishing, LLC , All Rights Reserved

BLIND SQUIRREL
PUBLISHING

Step By Step Walkthrough

Exporting Power View Dashboards To PowerPoint

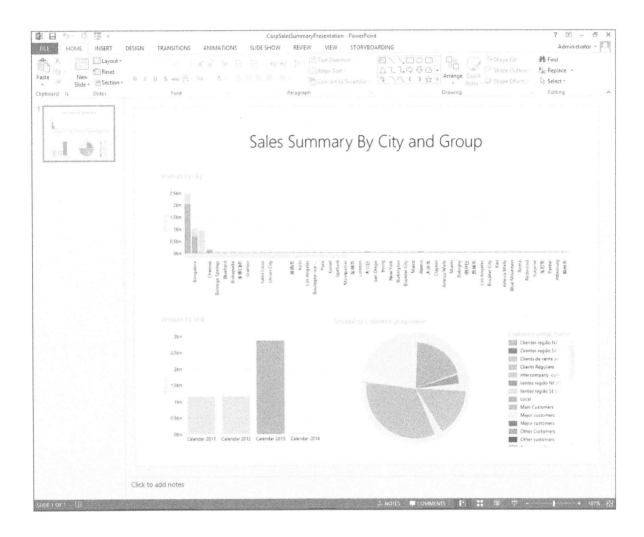

When the PowerPoint opens up you will see that the dashboard that you just created is now embedded within the slide.

Step By Step Walkthrough

Exporting Power View Dashboards To PowerPoint

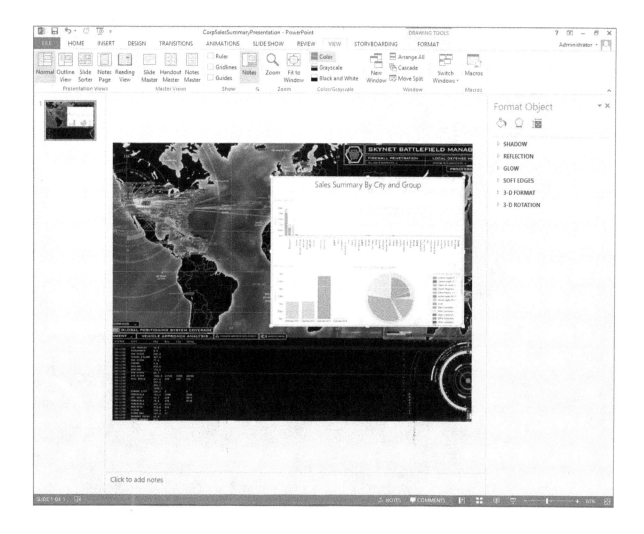

You can re-arrange the slide and add any additional embellishments and backgrounds that you like. Also notice that you can resize the dashboard itself.

daxc
www.dynamicsaxcompanions.com
Dynamics AX Companions

- 123 -

www.blindsquirrelpublishing.com
© 2015 Blind Squirrel Publishing, LLC , All Rights Reserved

BLIND SQUIRREL
PUBLISHING

Step By Step Walkthrough

Exporting Power View Dashboards To PowerPoint

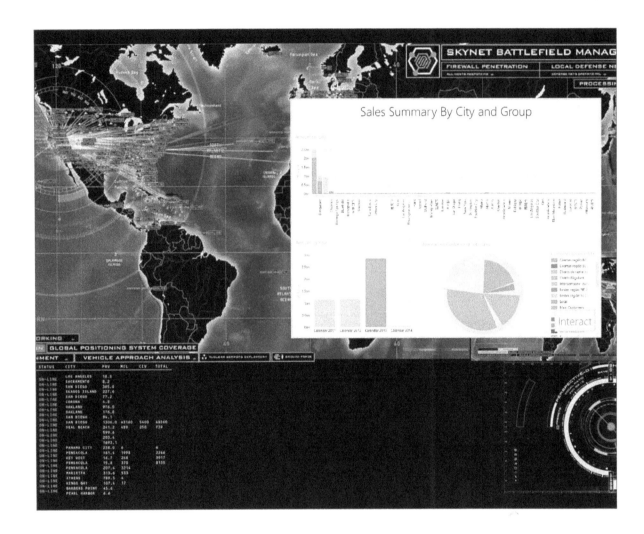

The real magic occurs when you switch to Slideshow mode. If you notice on the dashboard, there is an **INTERACT** button.

Step By Step Walkthrough

Exporting Power View Dashboards To PowerPoint

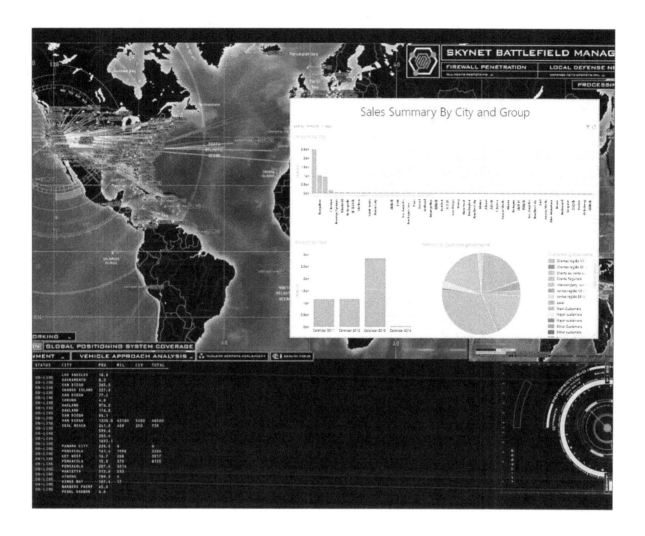

If you click on the **INTERACT** button the report becomes live getting data from the cube within the PowerPoint.

Step By Step Walkthrough

Exporting Power View Dashboards To PowerPoint

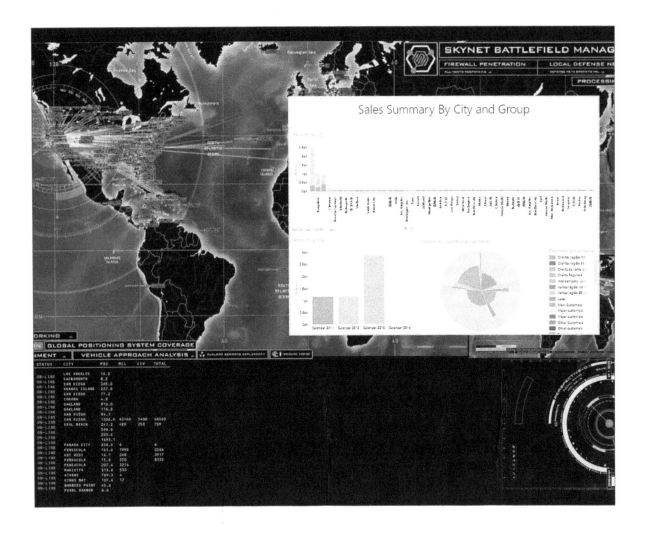

You can even click on any of the data and it will filter out the other views for you.

www.dynamicsaxcompanions.com
Dynamics AX Companions

- 126 -

www.blindsquirrelpublishing.com
© 2015 Blind Squirrel Publishing, LLC , All Rights Reserved

BLIND SQUIRREL
PUBLISHING

Adding Dashboards To Role Centers

Another option that you have with the web based Power View reports is to add them to your Role Center. This allows you to see them every time you log into Dynamics AX without having to launch a new windows or finding the reporting link.

daxc
www.dynamicsaxcompanions.com
Dynamics AX Companions

- 127 -

www.blindsquirrelpublishing.com
© 2015 Blind Squirrel Publishing, LLC, All Rights Reserved

BLIND SQUIRREL
PUBLISHING

Step By Step Walkthrough

Adding Dashboards To Role Centers

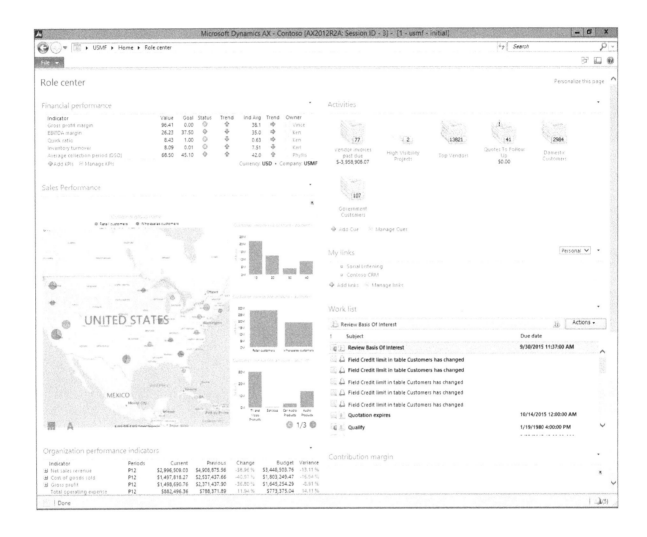

To add a Power View report to your Role Center, simply start off by clicking on the **Personalize The Site** link in the top right hand corner of your role center.

Step By Step Walkthrough

Adding Dashboards To Role Centers

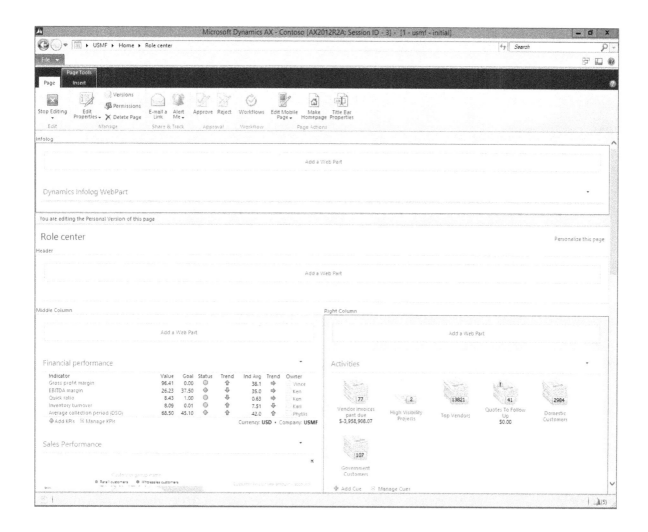

This will switch the view into the Personalization mode. Now click on the **Add a Web Part** link within the area of the page that you want to add the report into.

Step By Step Walkthrough

Adding Dashboards To Role Centers

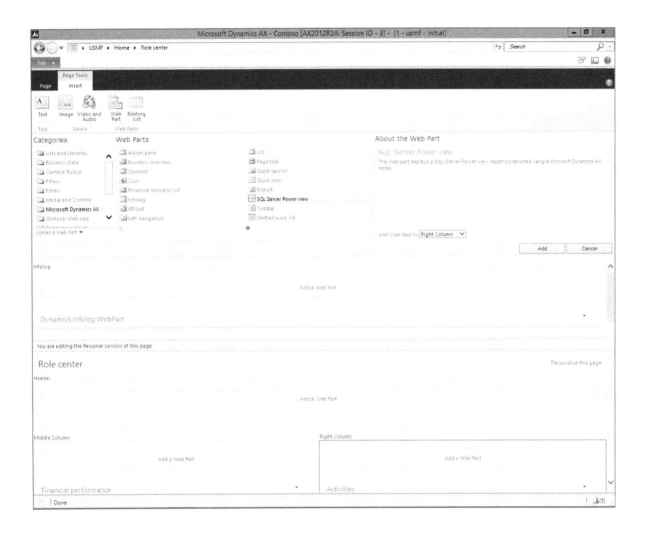

When the **Web Part Explorer** is displayed, select the **Microsoft Dynamics AX** category, select the **SQL Server Power View** web part and then click on the **Add** button to add the web part to the role center.

Step By Step Walkthrough

Adding Dashboards To Role Centers

When you return back to the web part layout manager you will be able to see a new web part is there called **SQL Server Power View**.

Step By Step Walkthrough

Adding Dashboards To Role Centers

Click on the options icon for the **SQL Server Power View** web part and select the **Edit My Web Part** menu item.

Step By Step Walkthrough

Adding Dashboards To Role Centers

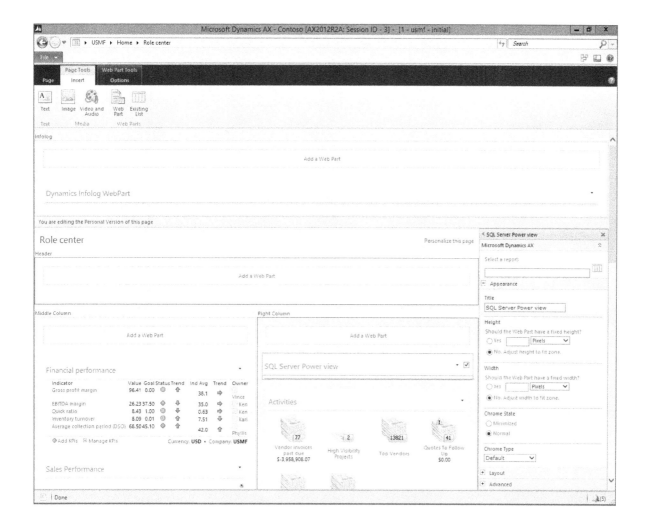

This will open up the properties window for the web part. Now we want to select the Power View report that we want to display in the form. To do this click on the orange grid icon to the right of the **Select A Report** property.

Step By Step Walkthrough

Adding Dashboards To Role Centers

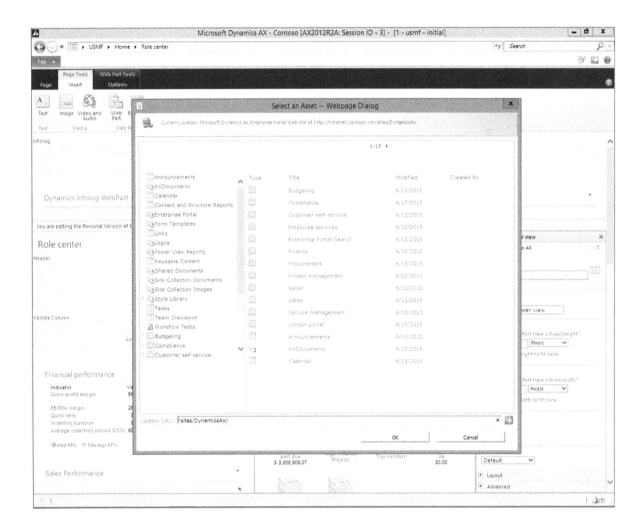

This will open up a SharePoint asset browser. To see all of the Power View reports select the **Power View Reports** asset group.

Step By Step Walkthrough

Adding Dashboards To Role Centers

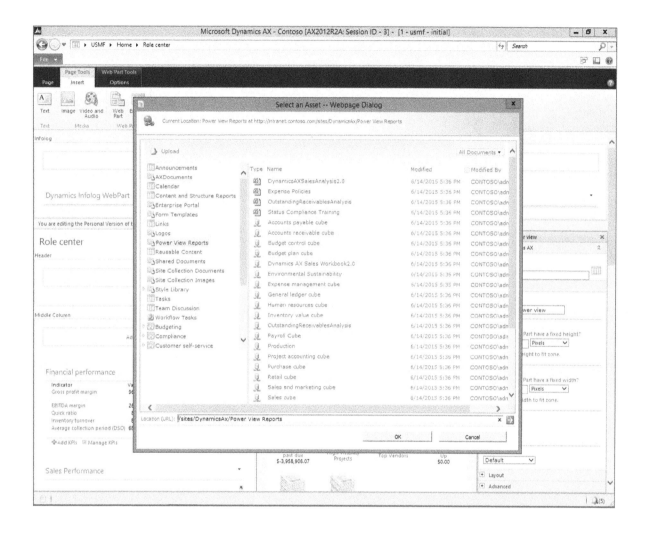

Now you will be able to see all of the different Power View reports and data sources that are available to select from.

Step By Step Walkthrough

Adding Dashboards To Role Centers

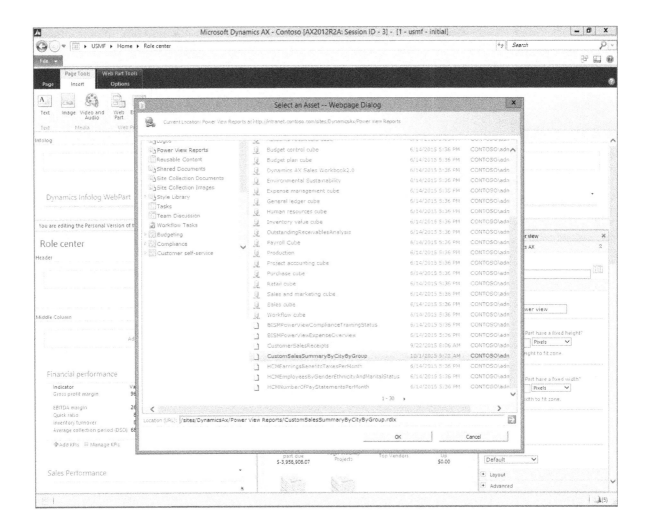

If you scroll down within the form you will be able to find the report that you just created. Select the form and then click on the **OK** button.

Step By Step Walkthrough

Adding Dashboards To Role Centers

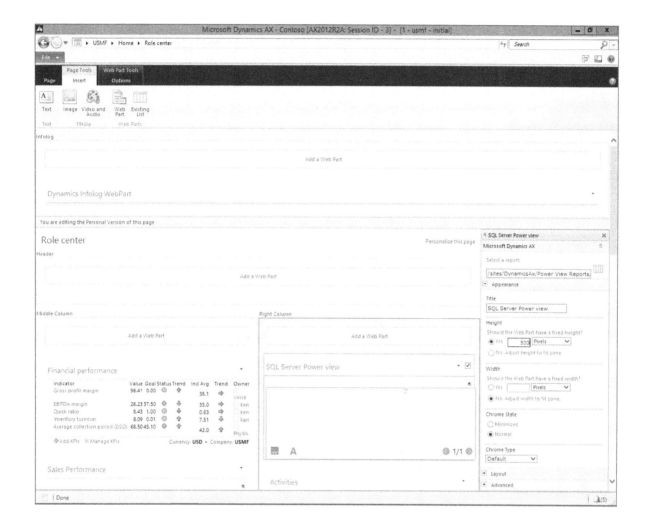

When you return back the **Select A Report** field will now have a link to your report. Within the **Height** field group, select the **Yes** option so that you can specify the height of the web part and select the Height to **500** pixels. If you don't do this then the report will lokk a little crunched.

daxc www.dynamicsaxcompanions.com
Dynamics AX Companions
- 137 -
www.blindsquirrelpublishing.com
© 2015 Blind Squirrel Publishing, LLC, All Rights Reserved
BLIND SQUIRREL
PUBLISHING

Step By Step Walkthrough

Adding Dashboards To Role Centers

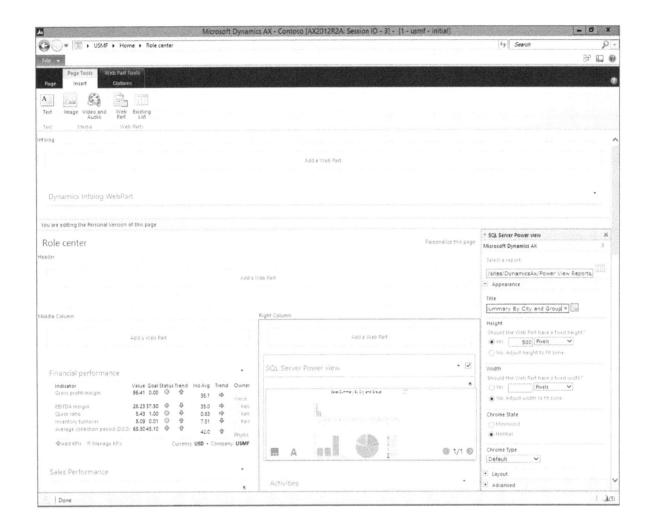

Also set the **Title** of the web part to **Sales Summary By City By Group** so that the boring default heading is overridden.

Step By Step Walkthrough

Adding Dashboards To Role Centers

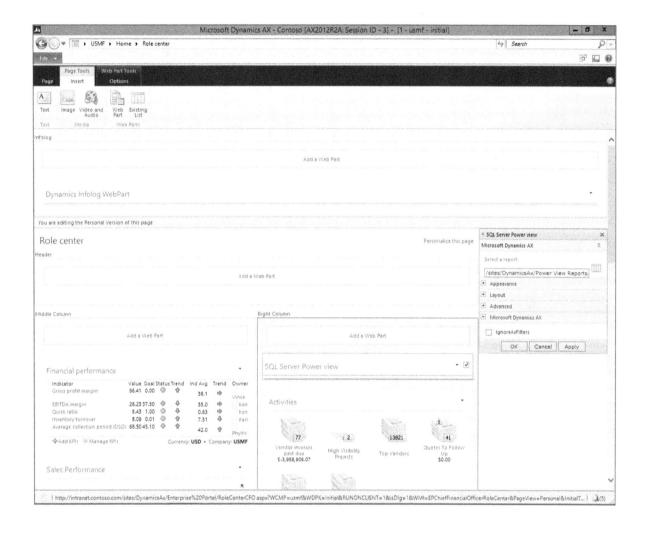

Finally, expand out the **Microsoft Dynamics AX** group and you will see that there is a single option there called **Ignore Filters**. If this is unchecked then the Web Part will automatically pass through the Company field as a parameter. If you don't have this defined in your report then the report will get a little confused.

Step By Step Walkthrough

Adding Dashboards To Role Centers

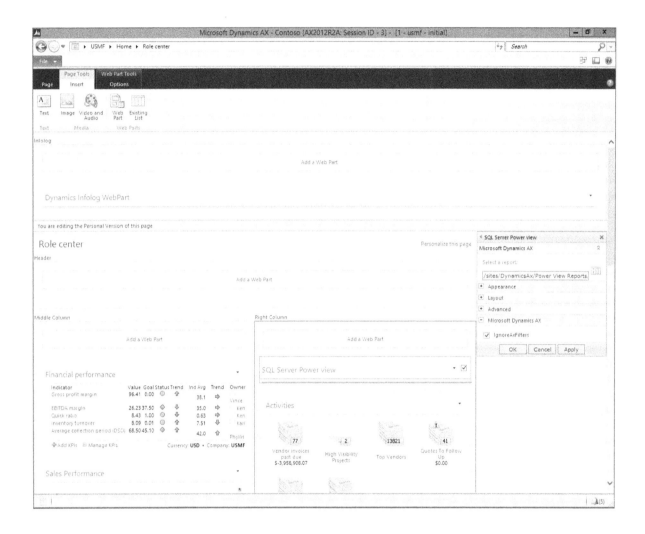

Check the **Ignore Filters** field and then click on the **OK** button.

Step By Step Walkthrough

Adding Dashboards To Role Centers

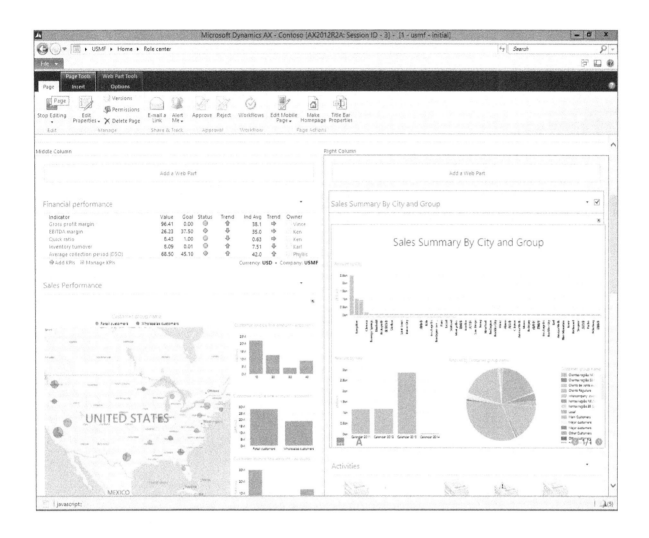

When you return back to the Role Center you will see the new report has been added for you.
All you need to do is click on the **Stop Editing** button in the **Page** ribbon bar to exit design more.

Step By Step Walkthrough

Adding Dashboards To Role Centers

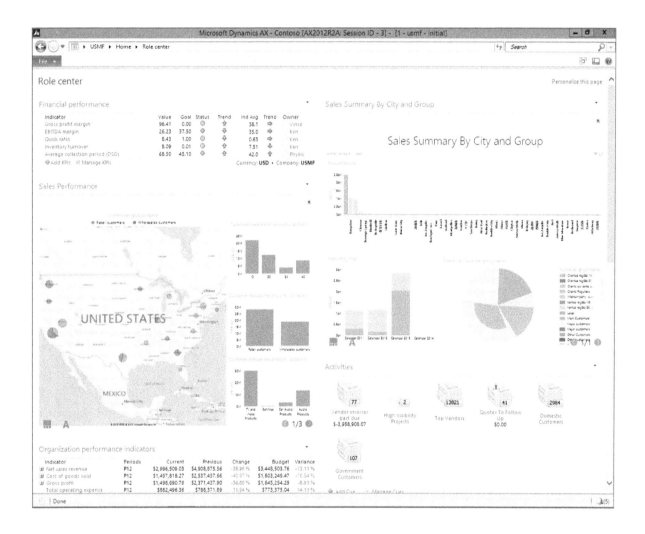

When you return back to the Role Center you will see that the report dashboard is not embedded within the Role Center and you can also filter the data just by selecting it.

Summary

In this presentation we have walked through a number of different ways that the users are able to use the tools that they have at their fingertips to create reports ranging from simple list pages, to SSRS style reports and then cleverer reports using Power View, Power Pivot and also the standard cubes that are delivered with Dynamics AX. All of this is done without having to ask IT to create a single report for you empowering the users to get information faster and also give them more options on the formatting and display.

daxc
www.dynamicsaxcompanions.com
Dynamics AX Companions

- 143 -

www.blindsquirrelpublishing.com
© 2015 Blind Squirrel Publishing, LLC, All Rights Reserved

BLIND SQUIRREL
PUBLISHING

SELF SERVICE REPORING USING POWER BI DESKTOP AND POWER BI ONLINE

Maybe you thought that the only thing that is better than Power BI within Excel is Power BI Online, but you are so wrong was wrong. The Power BI Desktop that is available within the Power hosted Power BI portal is much better and everyone needs to use it.

The Power BI Desktop is a standalone dashboard designing tool that takes all of the great features within Excel like Power Query, Power View, and Power Pivot and puts them in one single place to make all of your reporting a synch. And after you have finished building your dashboards, you can then publish them to the new hosted Power BI portal and create your own custom dashboards, and even perform Q&A on the data just by typing in the questions that you want answered.

In this chapter we will look at this new tool and how you can use it to quickly analyze all of your Dynamics AX data and also blend in multiple data feeds into one dashboard to view all of the data that you need all in one place.

 www.dynamicsaxcompanions.com
Dynamics AX Companions

- 145 -

www.blindsquirrelpublishing.com
© 2015 Blind Squirrel Publishing, LLC , All Rights Reserved

BLIND SQUIRREL
PUBLISHING

Signing Up for The Fremium Version of Power BI Online

You don't have to invest a lot of money in order to try out Power BI, in fact you don't have to spend any money at all. You can sign up for the personal version for **free**

daxc

www.dynamicsaxcompanions.com
Dynamics AX Companions

- 147 -

www.blindsquirrelpublishing.com
© 2015 Blind Squirrel Publishing, LLC , All Rights Reserved

BLIND SQUIRREL
PUBLISHING

Step By Step Walkthrough

Signing Up for The Fremium Version of Power BI Online

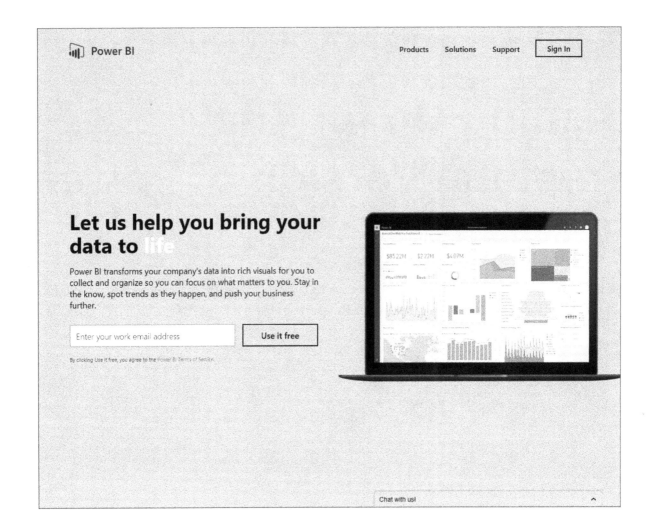

When you log into your Power BI site (www.Power BI.com), you will see that there is an option to **Use It Free**.

Step By Step Walkthrough

Signing Up For The Fremium Version of Power BI Online

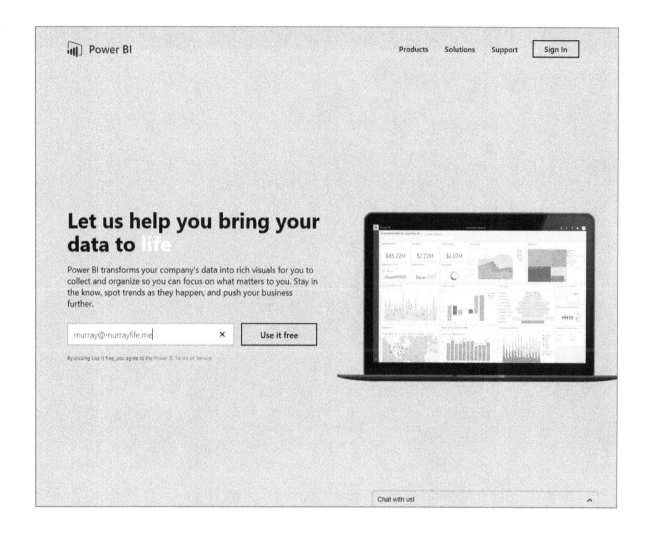

If you don't believe it, just type in yourO365 email account and click the button.

Step By Step Walkthrough

Signing Up For The Fremium Version of Power BI Online

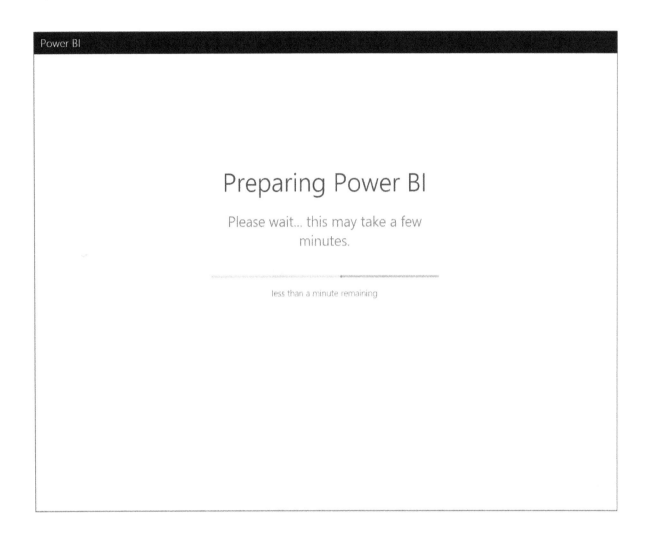

Power BI will then start hydrating your very own Power BI workspace...

 www.dynamicsaxcompanions.com
Dynamics AX Companions

- 150 -

www.blindsquirrelpublishing.com
© 2015 Blind Squirrel Publishing, LLC , All Rights Reserved

 BLIND SQUIRREL
PUBLISHING

Step By Step Walkthrough

Signing Up For The Fremium Version of Power BI Online

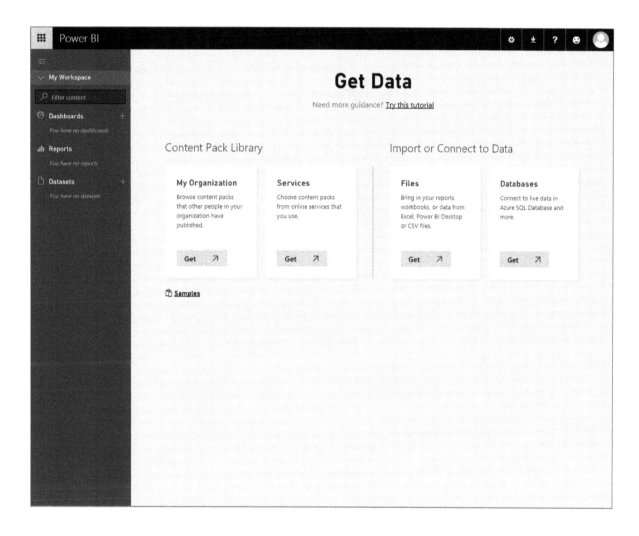

And within a couple of second you will have your own blank Power BI workspace.

Using the Preconfigured Dashboard Packages

Before we start creating our own dashboards and reports from our data, let's take a quick look at the Pre-configured packages that come with Power BI – you may not have to do any work at all...

Step By Step Walkthrough

Using the Preconfigured Dashboard Packages

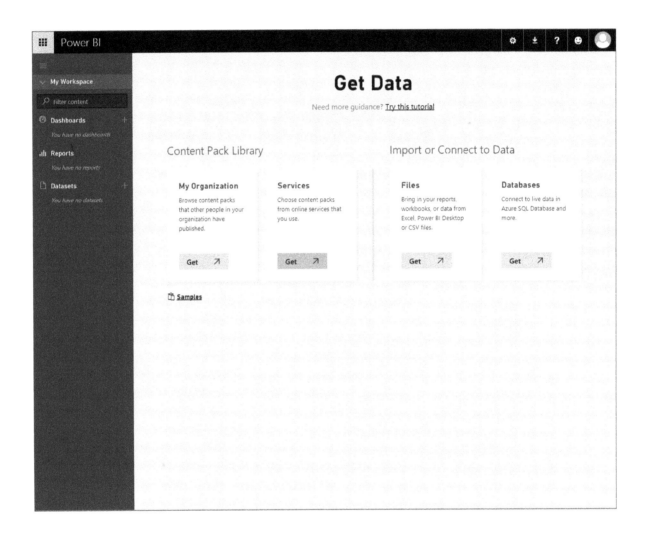

On the welcome screen for Power BI there are a number of different places that you can get data from. The **Services** is one of the most interesting.

Step By Step Walkthrough

Using the Preconfigured Dashboard Packages

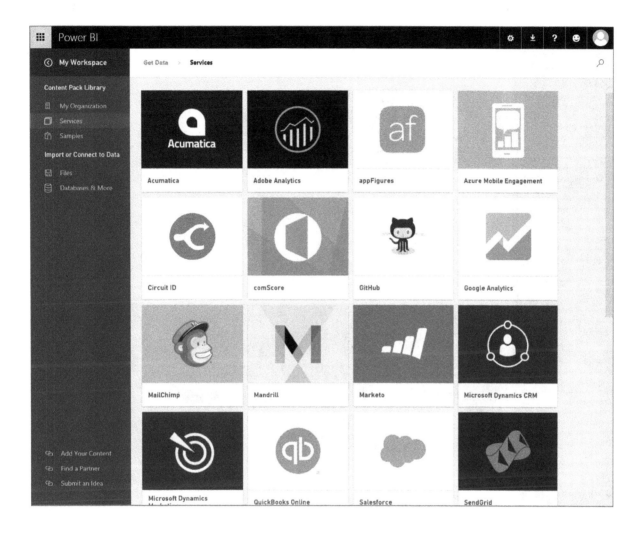

Within the **Services** data service you'll find a whole slew of different pre-configured dashboards that can be linked to different services. All they need is the connection information.

Step By Step Walkthrough

Using the Preconfigured Dashboard Packages

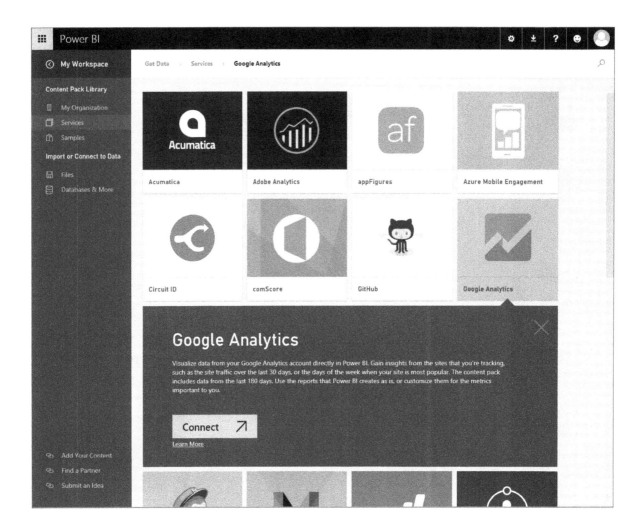

For example, we can connect to your own Google Analytics account.

Step By Step Walkthrough

Using the Preconfigured Dashboard Packages

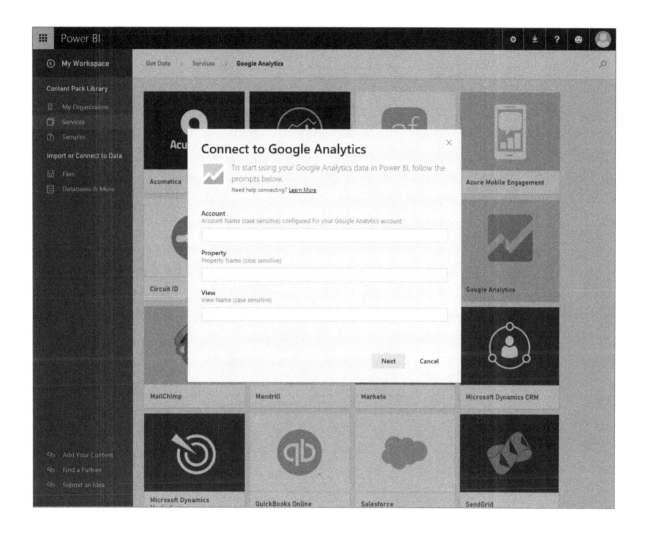

When you start the connection it will ask you for the connection information.

daxc   www.dynamicsaxcompanions.com
Dynamics AX Companions
- 157 -
www.blindsquirrelpublishing.com
© 2015 Blind Squirrel Publishing, LLC , All Rights Reserved
   BLIND SQUIRREL
PUBLISHING

Step By Step Walkthrough

Using the Preconfigured Dashboard Packages

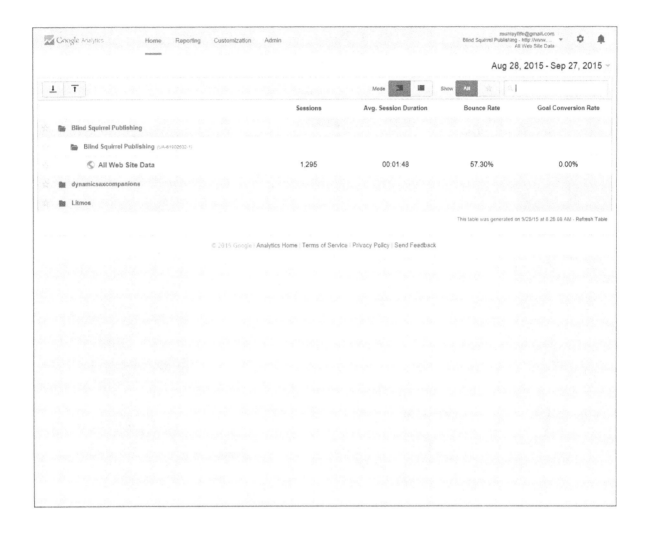

Here's the secret decoder ring for this option – the **Account, Property**, and **View** are just the three levels within your Google Analytics connection.

Step By Step Walkthrough

Using the Preconfigured Dashboard Packages

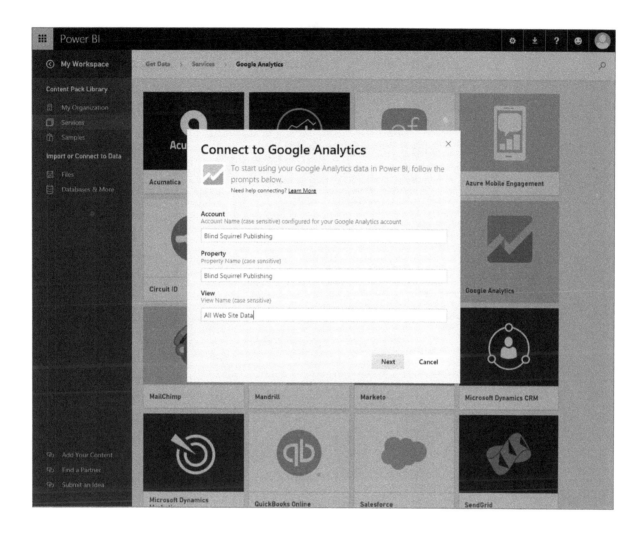

All you have to do is type in the connection information (this is case sensitive) and click on the **Next** button.

Step By Step Walkthrough

Using the Preconfigured Dashboard Packages

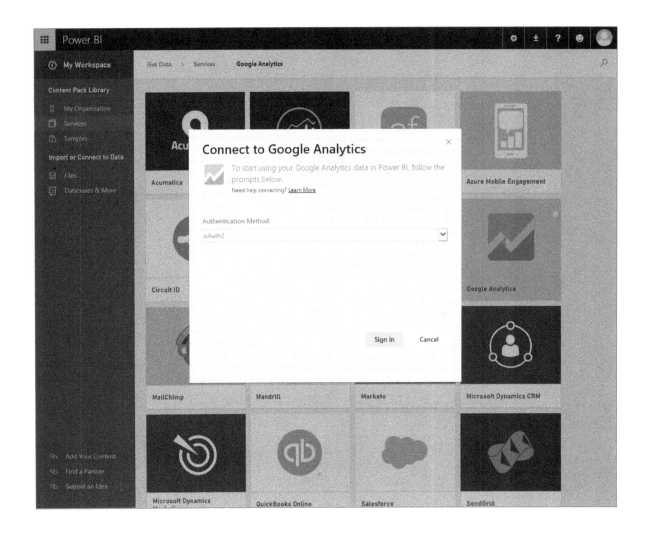

Then you will be asked to sign in with your credentials using the oAuth2 protocol.

Step By Step Walkthrough

Using the Preconfigured Dashboard Packages

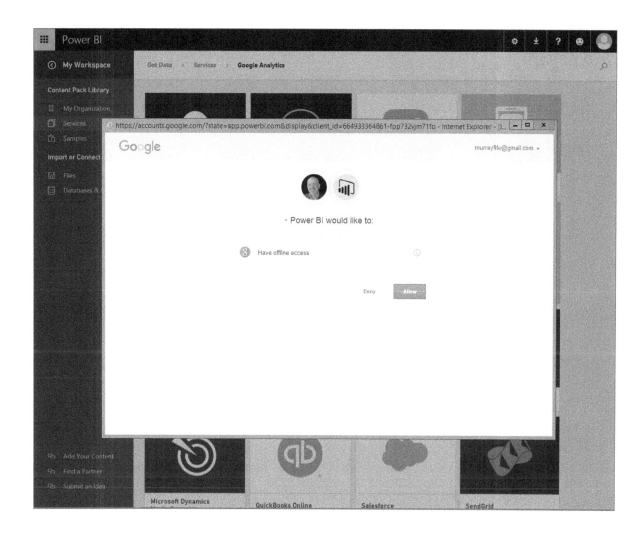

After you have done that you just authorize the connection between the services.

Step By Step Walkthrough

Using the Preconfigured Dashboard Packages

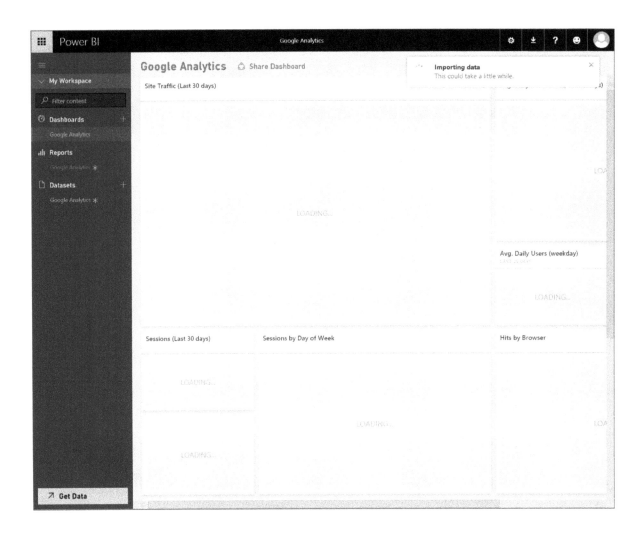

After you have done that you will be taken to a pre-configured dashboard for that service and Power BI will start hydrating the dashboards with your data.

 www.dynamicsaxcompanions.com
Dynamics AX Companions
- 162 -
www.blindsquirrelpublishing.com
© 2015 Blind Squirrel Publishing, LLC , All Rights Reserved
BLIND SQUIRREL
PUBLISHING

Step By Step Walkthrough

Using the Preconfigured Dashboard Packages

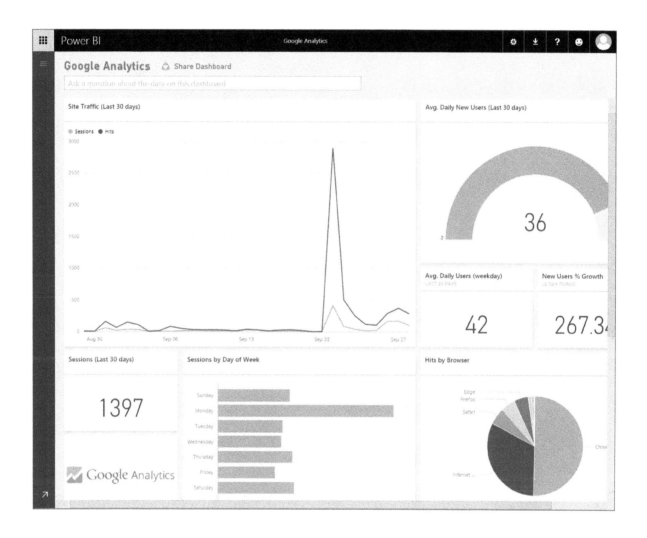

Within a couple of seconds you will have a fully loaded analytics Dashboard and you didn't even have to break a sweat.

www.dynamicsaxcompanions.com
Dynamics AX Companions

- 163 -

www.blindsquirrelpublishing.com
© 2015 Blind Squirrel Publishing, LLC , All Rights Reserved

BLIND SQUIRREL
PUBLISHING

Downloading The Power BI Desktop Application

Although you can get data directly from within Power BI Online and generate your dashboards, there is a much easier way to create your dashboards on your desktop using the Power BI Desktop Application. And it's free to download as well.

daxc   www.dynamicsaxcompanions.com
Dynamics AX Companions

- 165 -

www.blindsquirrelpublishing.com
© 2015 Blind Squirrel Publishing, LLC , All Rights Reserved

BLIND SQUIRREL
PUBLISHING

Step By Step Walkthrough

Downloading The Power BI Desktop Application

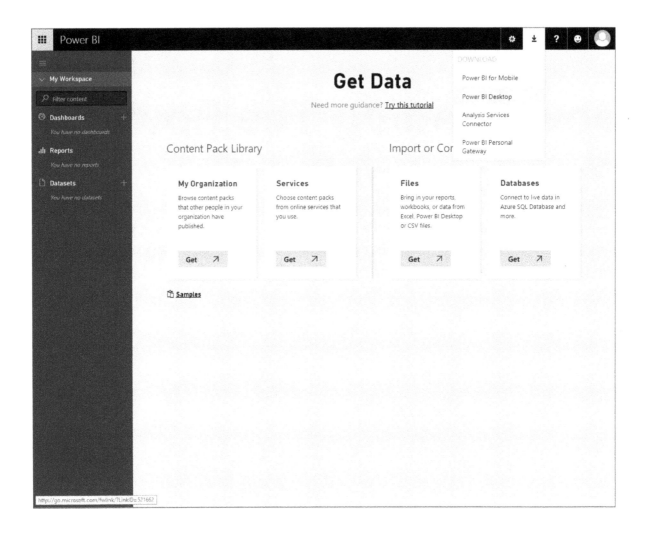

To get your copy, just click on the dropdown icon in the top right of the **Power BI Online** website and you will see an option to get the **Power BI Desktop**

Step By Step Walkthrough

Downloading The Power BI Desktop Application

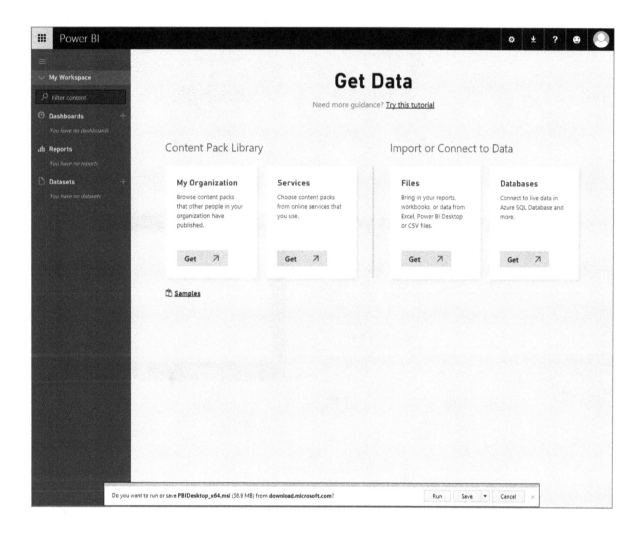

If you click on it then you will be able to download the install files.

Step By Step Walkthrough

Downloading The Power BI Desktop Application

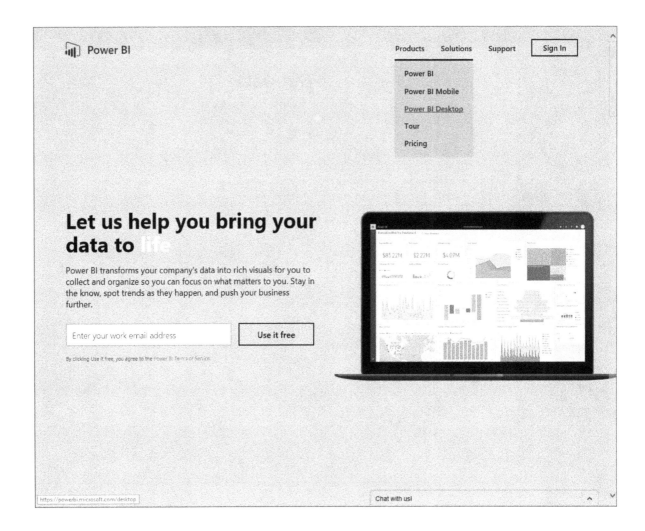

Alternatively you can go to **powerbi.com** site and click on the **Power BI Desktop** link within the **Products** dropdown menu.

daxc

www.dynamicsaxcompanions.com
Dynamics AX Companions

- 168 -

www.blindsquirrelpublishing.com
© 2015 Blind Squirrel Publishing, LLC, All Rights Reserved

BLIND SQUIRREL
PUBLISHING

Step By Step Walkthrough

Downloading The Power BI Desktop Application

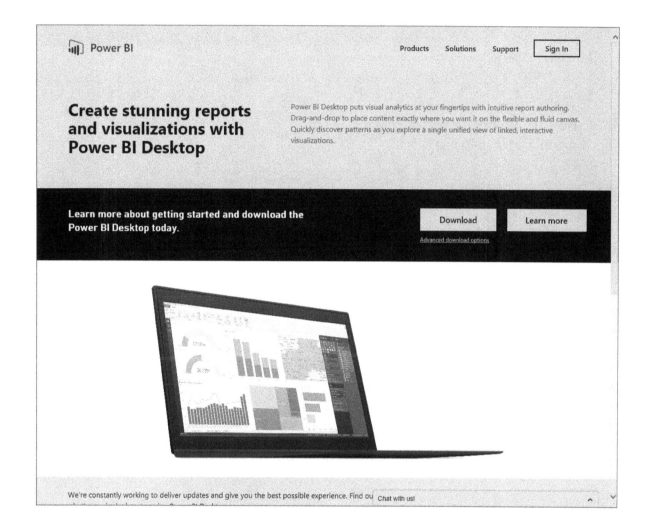

That will take you to the product page and you will be able to download the install files from there as well.

daxc

www.dynamicsaxcompanions.com
Dynamics AX Companions

- 169 -

www.blindsquirrelpublishing.com
© 2015 Blind Squirrel Publishing, LLC , All Rights Reserved

BLIND SQUIRREL
PUBLISHING

Step By Step Walkthrough

Downloading The Power BI Desktop Application

All you have to do is click through the welcome page...

Step By Step Walkthrough

Downloading The Power BI Desktop Application

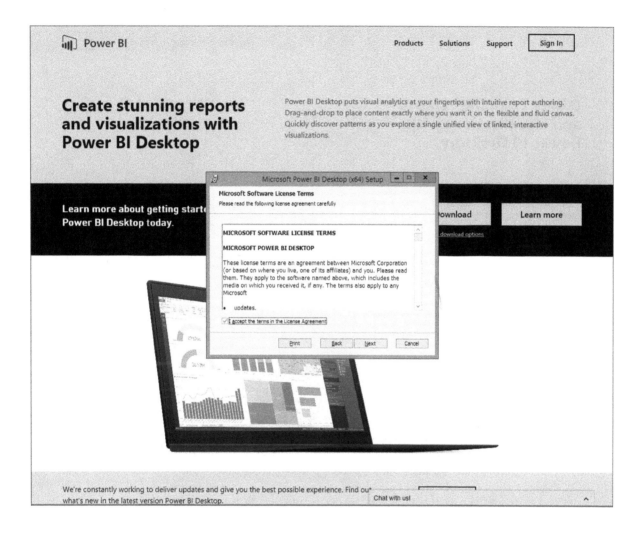

Accept the obligatory license agreement...

www.dynamicsaxcompanions.com
Dynamics AX Companions

- 171 -

www.blindsquirrelpublishing.com
© 2015 Blind Squirrel Publishing, LLC, All Rights Reserved

BLIND SQUIRREL
PUBLISHING

Step By Step Walkthrough

Downloading The Power BI Desktop Application

Tell it where to install...

www.blindsquirrelpublishing.com
© 2015 Blind Squirrel Publishing, LLC , All Rights Reserved

BLIND SQUIRREL
PUBLISHING

Step By Step Walkthrough

Downloading The Power BI Desktop Application

And click **Install**.

Step By Step Walkthrough

Downloading The Power BI Desktop Application

After it is done, click on the **Finish** button and your are done.

Step By Step Walkthrough

Downloading The Power BI Desktop Application

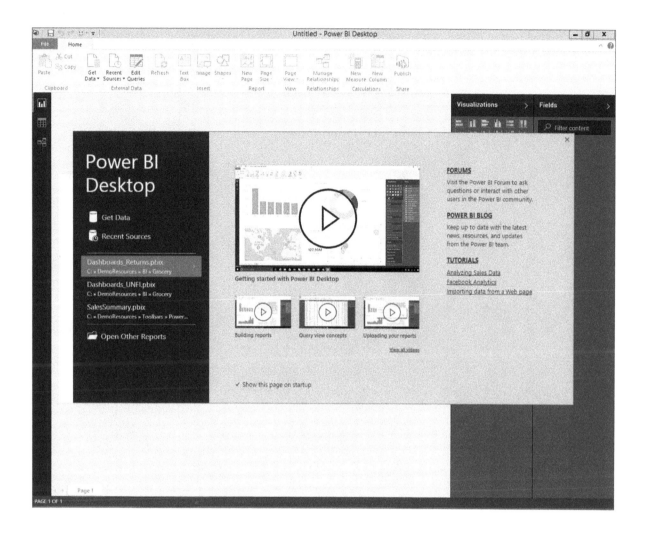

The next thing that you know the Power BI Desktop application will be waiting for you to start plundering some data.

Getting Your Reporting Data Into Power BI

Now that you have Power BI Desktop installed you can start getting some data to report off.

www.dynamicsaxcompanions.com
Dynamics AX Companions

- 177 -

Step By Step Walkthrough

Getting Your Reporting Data Into Power BI

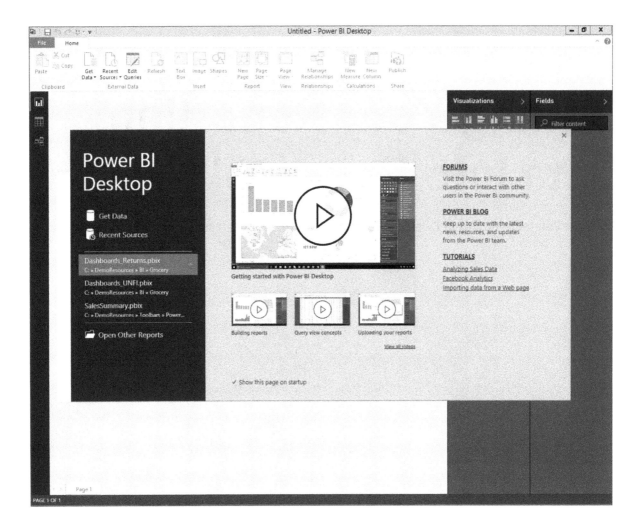

To start off you can just click on the **Get Data** option.

Step By Step Walkthrough

Getting Your Reporting Data Into Power BI

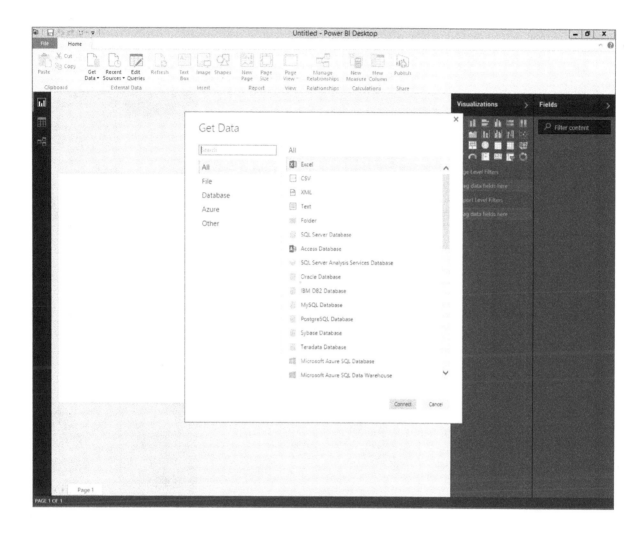

This will open up a dialog box with all of the different data sources that you can connect to for your dashboard. For this example we've extracted data out into an Excel workbook so we will use the **Excel** option.

Step By Step Walkthrough

Getting Your Reporting Data Into Power BI

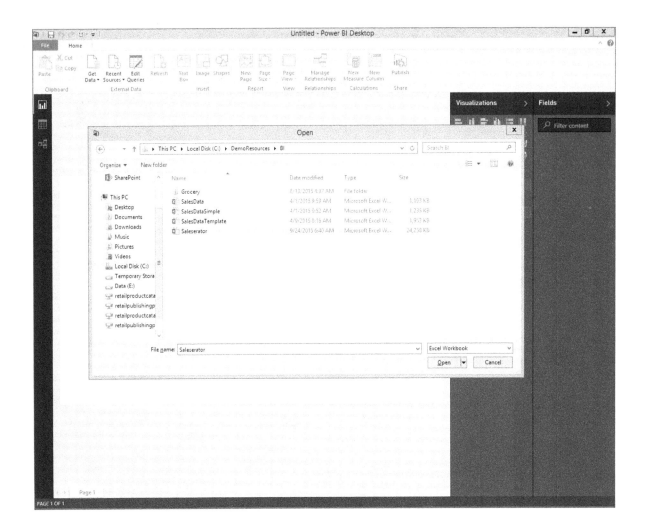

When the file explorer is displayed, select the data that you want to use as the data source and then click on the **Open** button.

Tip: To get a copy of the sample data use this link: https://doc.co/sjuSP1

Step By Step Walkthrough

Getting Your Reporting Data Into Power BI

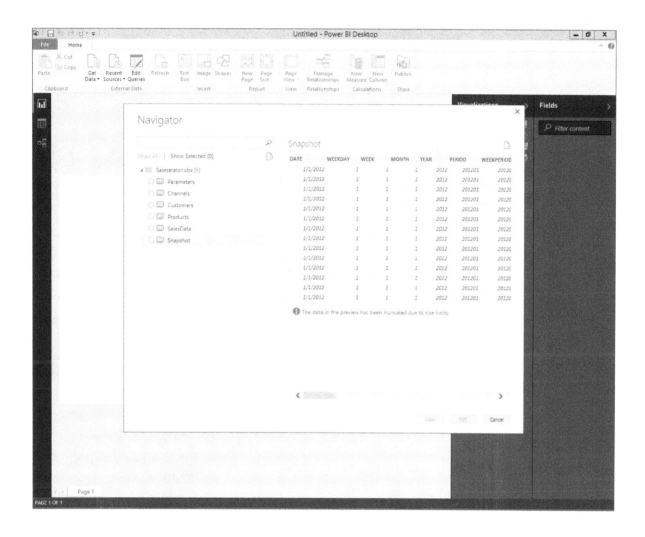

This will open up a Navigator showing you all of the different sheets that are available within the workbook.

Step By Step Walkthrough

Getting Your Reporting Data Into Power BI

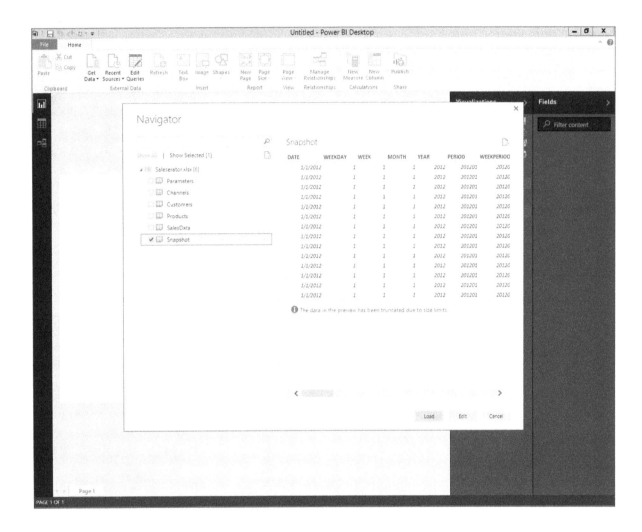

Just select the one with all of the data that you want to report off and click on the **Load** button.

daxc
www.dynamicsaxcompanions.com
Dynamics AX Companions

- 182 -

www.blindsquirrelpublishing.com
© 2015 Blind Squirrel Publishing, LLC , All Rights Reserved

BLIND SQUIRREL
PUBLISHING

Step By Step Walkthrough

Getting Your Reporting Data Into Power BI

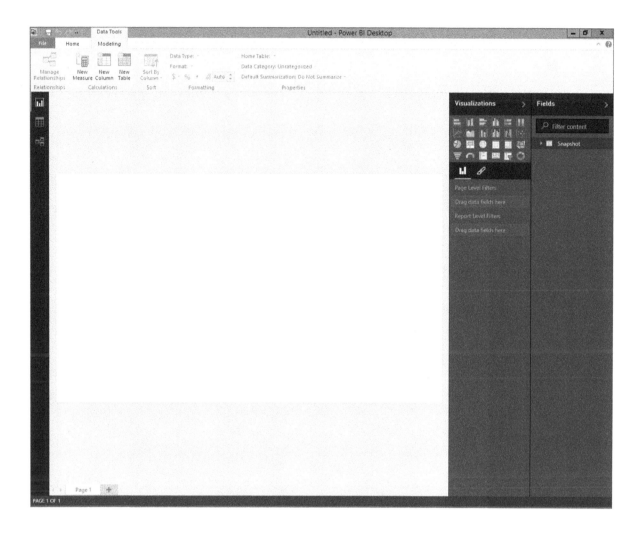

Next thing you know you will be taken to a dashboard designer workspace and your data connection will be shown in the fields panel on the right.

Using The Report View To Create Dashboards

Now that you have the data loaded you might as well start creating some dashboards with it.

www.dynamicsaxcompanions.com
Dynamics AX Companions

- 185 -

www.blindsquirrelpublishing.com
© 2015 Blind Squirrel Publishing, LLC , All Rights Reserved
BLIND SQUIRREL
PUBLISHING

Step By Step Walkthrough

Using The Report View To Create Dashboards

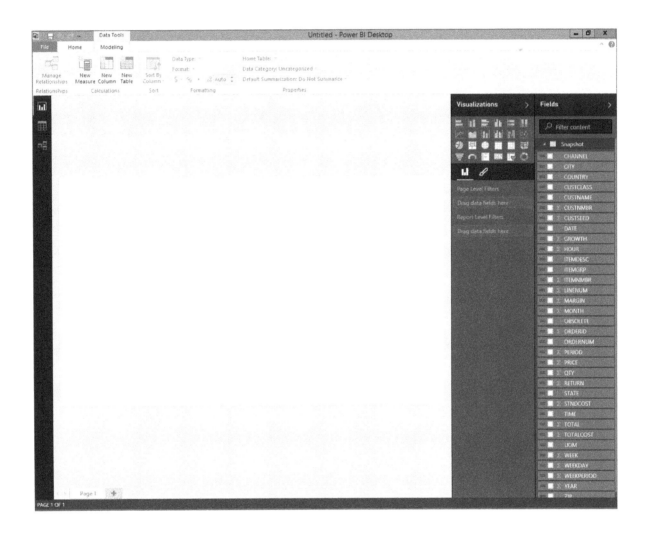

If you expand out the fields within the Field panel you will see all of the columns from the worksheet are available for you to report off.

Step By Step Walkthrough

Using The Report View To Create Dashboards

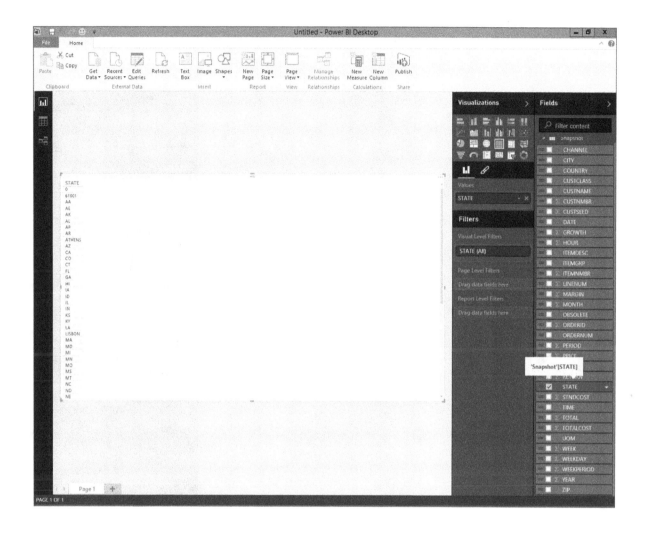

Now we can start building our dashboard. We will start off by selecting the **STATE** field and it will be added directly to the canvas.

Step By Step Walkthrough

Using The Report View To Create Dashboards

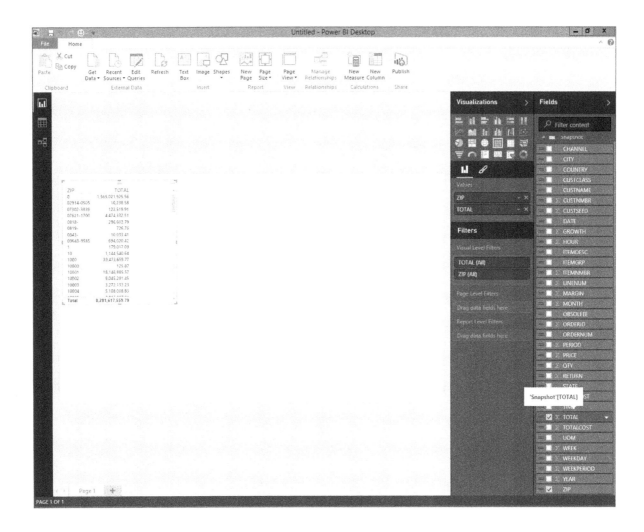

Next we can add a measure to the report, so click on the **TOTAL** field from the field chooser.

daxc
www.dynamicsaxcompanions.com
Dynamics AX Companions

- 188 -

www.blindsquirrelpublishing.com
© 2015 Blind Squirrel Publishing, LLC, All Rights Reserved

BLIND SQUIRREL
PUBLISHING

Step By Step Walkthrough

Using The Report View To Create Dashboards

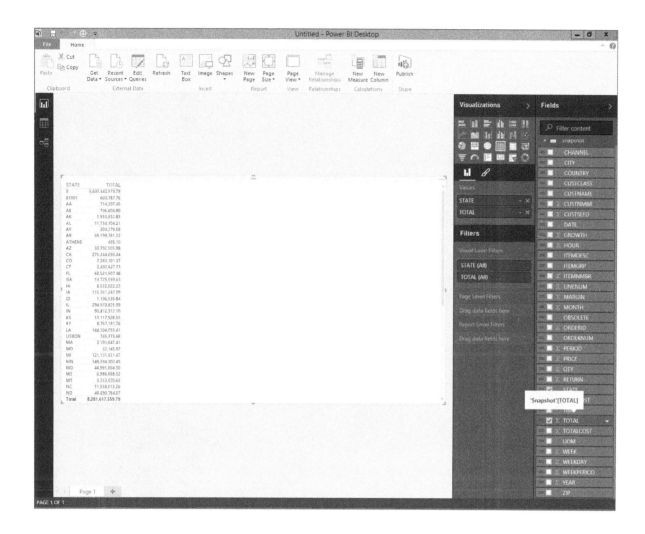

If you want to resize the table then you can just grab the edges of the table and drag them out to the boundaries of the canvas.

daxc
www.dynamicsaxcompanions.com
Dynamics AX Companions

- 189 -

www.blindsquirrelpublishing.com
© 2015 Blind Squirrel Publishing, LLC , All Rights Reserved

BLIND SQUIRREL
PUBLISHING

Step By Step Walkthrough

Using The Report View To Create Dashboards

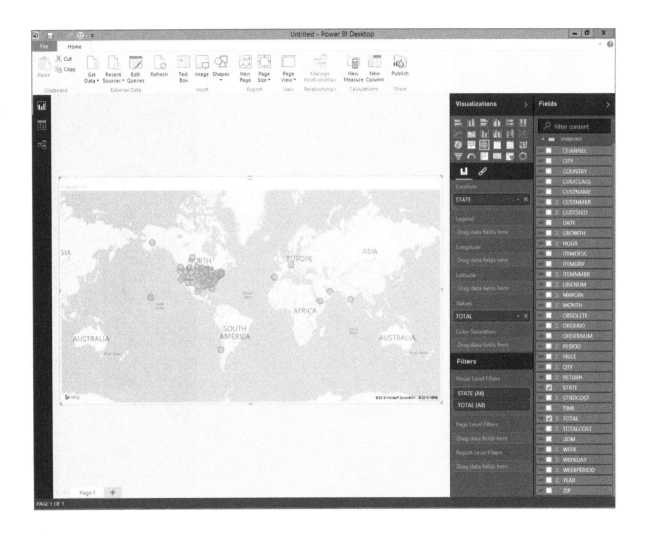

You will notice in the **Visualizations** panel there are a lot of different ways that we can look at the data. If you click on the icon that looks like a globe then the report will change to show you all of the sales by state as a map.

Step By Step Walkthrough

Using The Report View To Create Dashboards

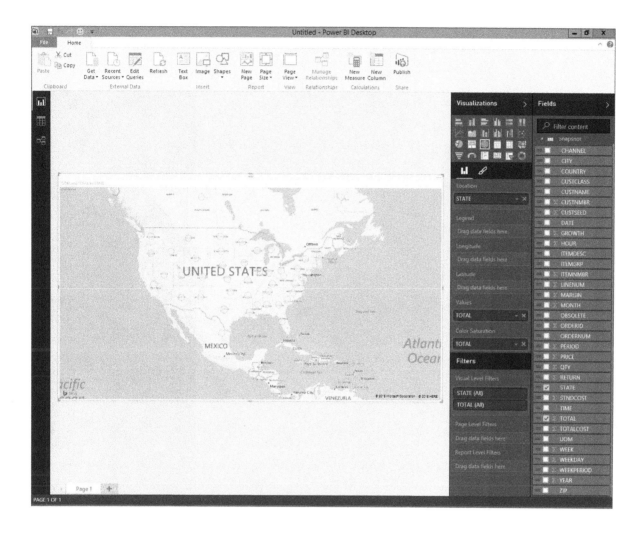

You can also change the visualization of the totals for each of the states now by adding a measure field to the **Color Saturation** field. To do this just drag the **TOTAL** field over to the **Color Saturation** field in the **Visualizations** panel.

daxc www.dynamicsaxcompanions.com
Dynamics AX Companions

- 191 -

www.blindsquirrelpublishing.com
© 2015 Blind Squirrel Publishing, LLC , All Rights Reserved

BLIND SQUIRREL
PUBLISHING

Step By Step Walkthrough

Using The Report View To Create Dashboards

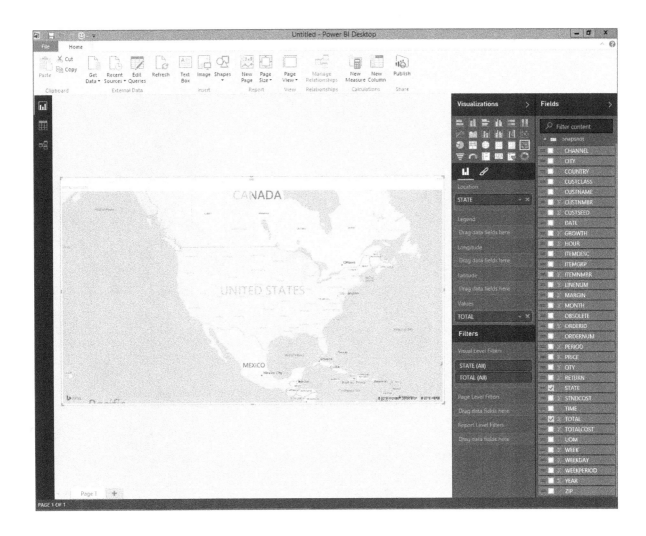

As an alternative way to vies the mapped data, click on the icon in the visualization that looks like a checkerboard map. This will change the view from dots for each of the states to colored sections.

Accessing The Query Editor

You may have noticed a couple of things that don't quite look right with the data fields that were created during the loading of the data. Some of the dimensions have been marked as measures and also the names look a little too loud since they are all in upper case.

Don't worry, PowerBI has a Query Editor that allows you to tidy up the data.

www.dynamicsaxcompanions.com
Dynamics AX Companions

- 193 -

www.blindsquirrelpublishing.com
© 2015 Blind Squirrel Publishing, LLC, All Rights Reserved

BLIND SQUIRREL
PUBLISHING

Step By Step Walkthrough

Accessing The Query Editor

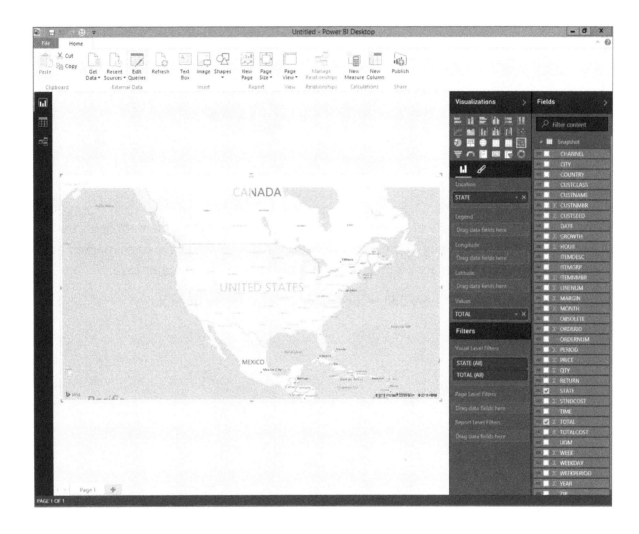

To access the **Query Editor** just click on the **Edit Query** button within the **External Data** button group of the **Home** ribbon bar.

Step By Step Walkthrough

Accessing The Query Editor

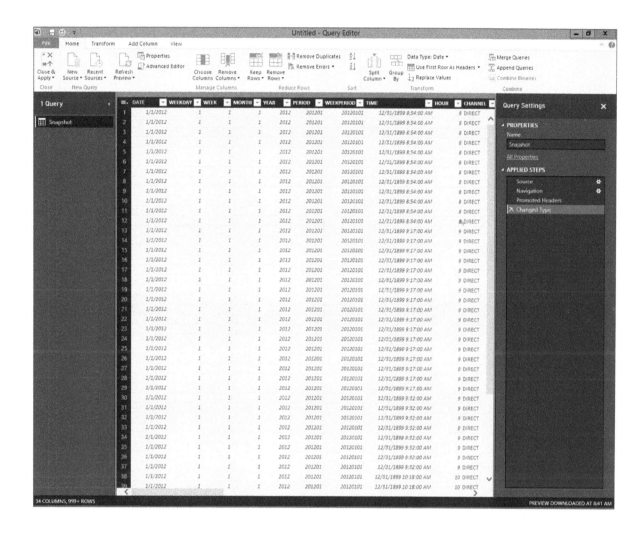

This will open up the **Query Editor** and you will see all of the data that you list loaded is displayed in a grid.

Changing Data's Data Types Through The Query Editor

Now that we are in the **Query Editor** we can start polishing up the data. To start off, lets change the datatypes of the columns of data so that they can be charted correctly by PowerBI

daxc

www.dynamicsaxcompanions.com
Dynamics AX Companions

- 197 -

www.blindsquirrelpublishing.com
© 2015 Blind Squirrel Publishing, LLC , All Rights Reserved

BLIND SQUIRREL
PUBLISHING

Step By Step Walkthrough
Changing Data's Data Types Through The Query Editor

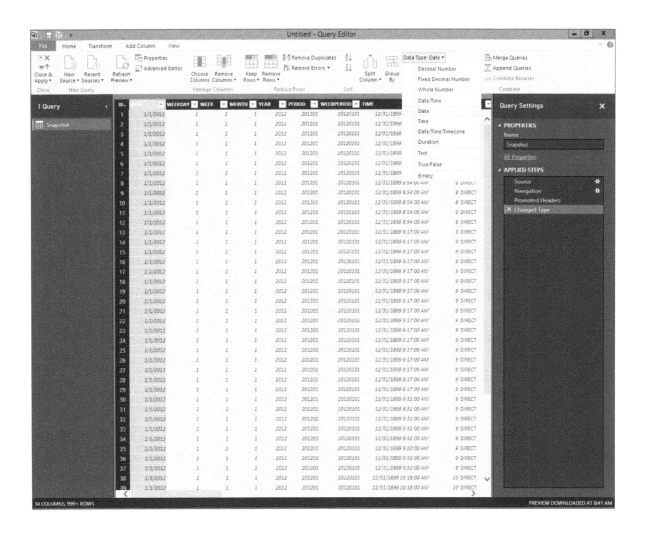

If you select any of the columns then you are able to change the datatype of the column from the default that was guessed by Power BI when it imported the data. For example, if you click on the **DATE** field then you will be able to click on the **Data Type** button in the ribbon bar and select the **Date** data type.

Step By Step Walkthrough

Changing Data's Data Types Through The Query Editor

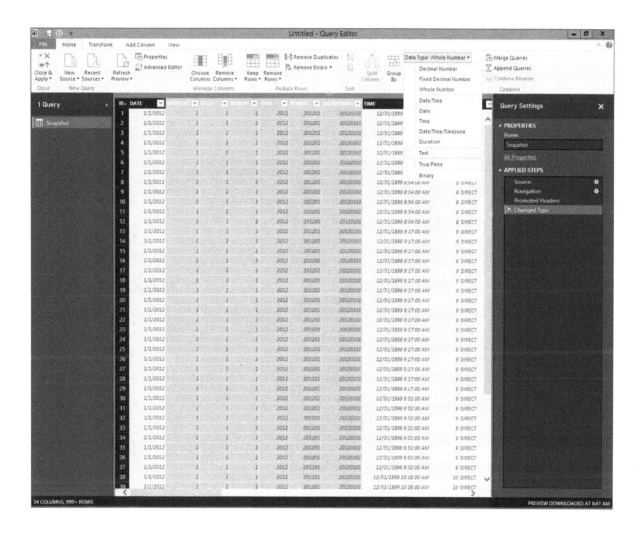

In this example, there are a lot of fields that are showing up as numerical fields when in fact they should be treated as text. Numerical fields are usually summed up by Power BI where as Text fields are more dimensional. So in this example we select all of the fields that are numbers and then click on the **Data Type** dropdown list and mark them as **Text**.

daxc
www.dynamicsaxcompanions.com
Dynamics AX Companions
- 199 -
www.blindsquirrelpublishing.com
© 2015 Blind Squirrel Publishing, LLC , All Rights Reserved
BLIND SQUIRREL
PUBLISHING

Step By Step Walkthrough

Changing Data's Data Types Through The Query Editor

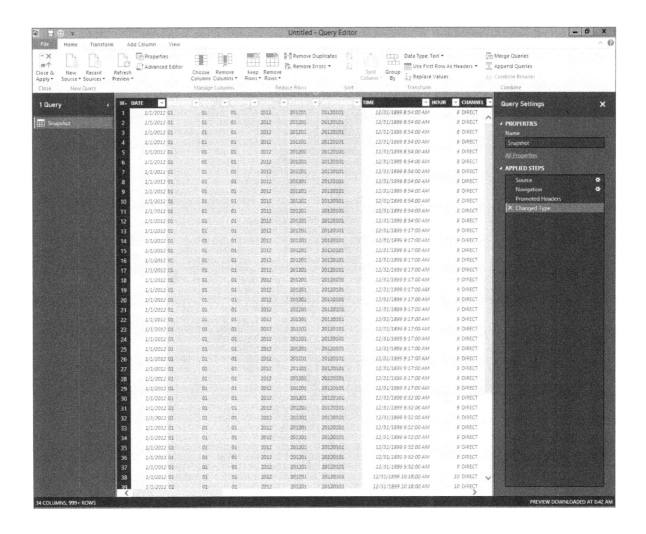

Now you will notice that all of the fields are showing up as text – the tell tale sign is that they are all left justified.

Step By Step Walkthrough

Changing Data's Data Types Through The Query Editor

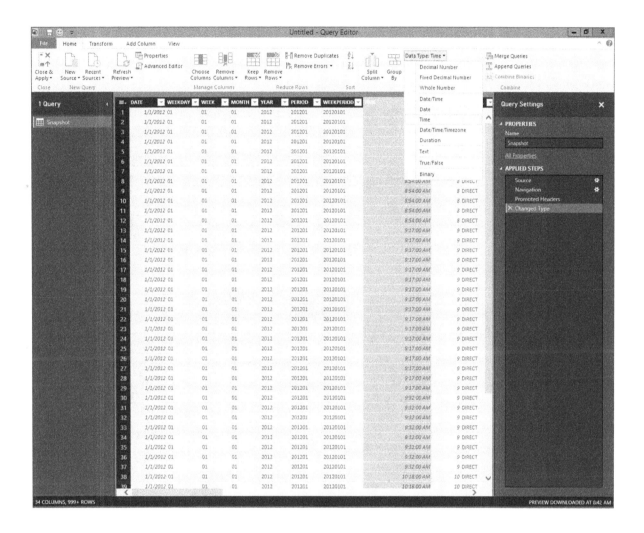

Next we will also select the **TIME** field and change it's data type to **Time** to make it a little more concise.

Step By Step Walkthrough

Changing Data's Data Types Through The Query Editor

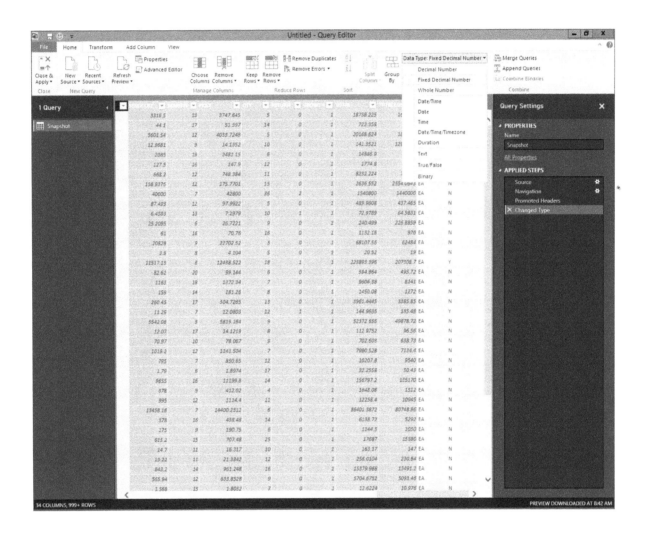

If we scroll further over into the data then we will also see a number of fields that are currency based. To tidy up the data we will change their data type to **Fixed Decimal Number** to get them ready to be marked as currency.

Step By Step Walkthrough

Changing Data's Data Types Through The Query Editor

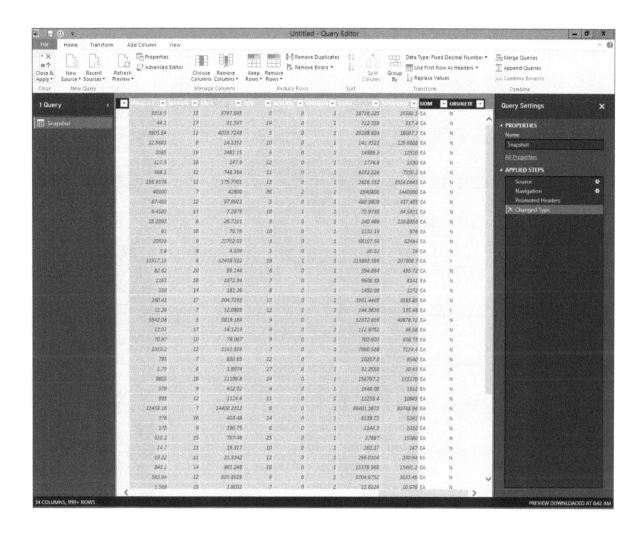

Now we have made these updates all of the fields should have the right datatype associated with them. One thing to point out at this point is that the Query Editor is tracking all of these changes for us and if you look over in the **Applied Steps** section of the Query Editor then you will see that there is a new step there called **Changed Type** which is storing all of these changes.

Step By Step Walkthrough

Changing Data's Data Types Through The Query Editor

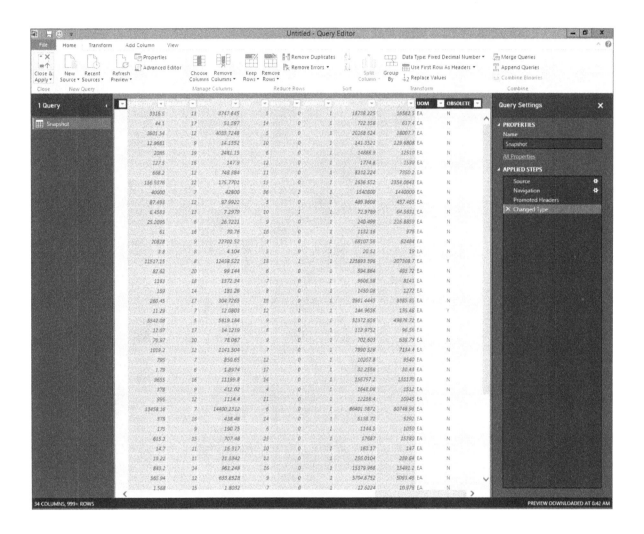

Now that we have made the changes to the query we can just click on the **Close & Apply** button to save the changes and return back to the main page of the designer.

Accessing The Data Editor

Power BI Desktop is really a number of tools in one. So far we have seen the dashboard designer and the query editor, but if you really want to polish up the data and make it look more friendly to the user then you will want to look at the **Data Editor**.

dαℵc
www.dynamicsaxcompanions.com
Dynamics AX Companions
- 205 -
www.blindsquirrelpublishing.com
© 2015 Blind Squirrel Publishing, LLC , All Rights Reserved
BLIND SQUIRREL
PUBLISHING

Step By Step Walkthrough

Accessing The Data Editor

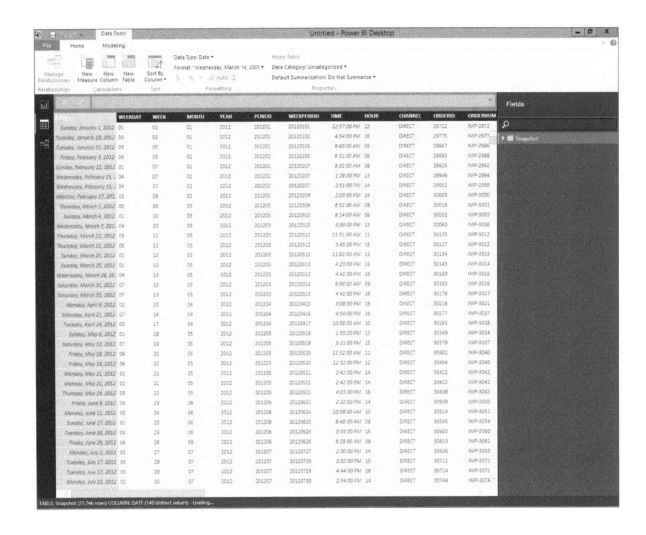

To switch to the **Data Editor** view all you need to do is click on the icon on the left hand side of the application.

Using The Data Editor To Change Data Types

Through the Query Editor we changed some of the field data types, but the Data Editor gives us a number of other ways that we can format the data types.

daxc
www.dynamicsaxcompanions.com
Dynamics AX Companions

- 207 -

BLIND SQUIRREL
PUBLISHING

Step By Step Walkthrough

Using The Data Editor To Change Data Types

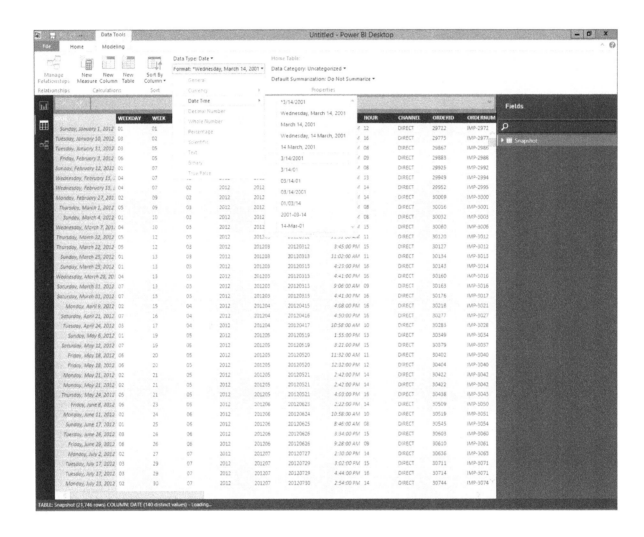

To start off if we look at the **DATE** field, there is a little too much information that is showing. All we really want is the simple date. So if we select the **DATE** column we can then click on the **Format** dropdown, select the **Date Time** option and then choose a short date format.

Step By Step Walkthrough

Using The Data Editor To Change Data Types

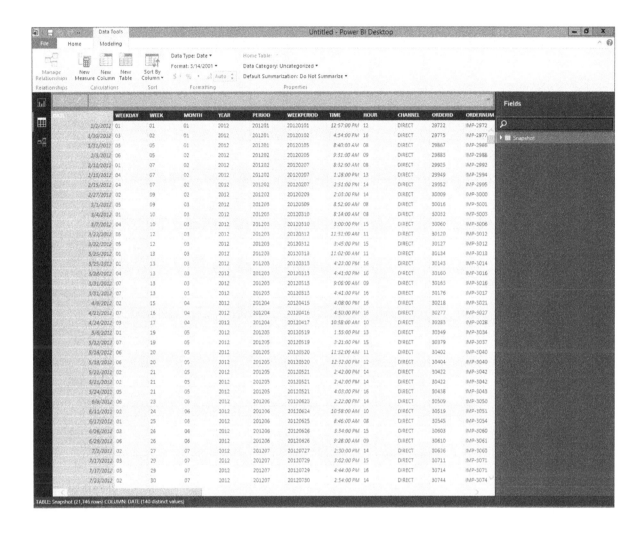

Now you will see that the **DATE** data is formatted in the more concise way.

 www.dynamicsaxcompanions.com
Dynamics AX Companions

- 209 -

www.blindsquirrelpublishing.com
© 2015 Blind Squirrel Publishing, LLC , All Rights Reserved

BLIND SQUIRREL
PUBLISHING

Step By Step Walkthrough

Using The Data Editor To Change Data Types

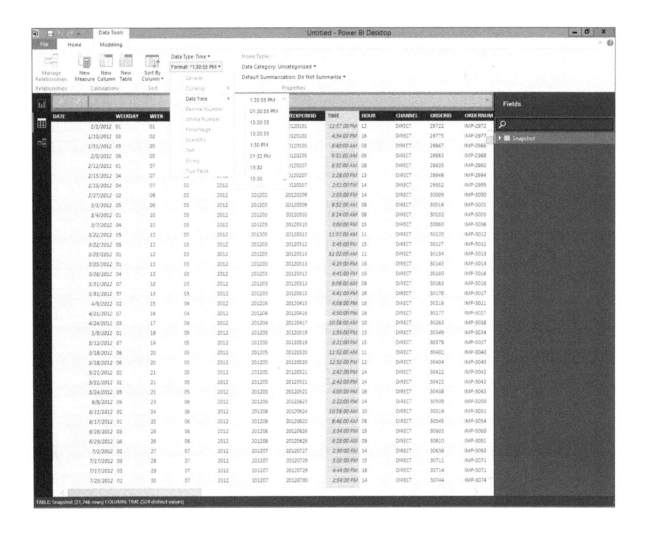

We can also change the format of the **TIME** field as well, and make it military time. This will allow us to graph the time more accurately without any sorting errors.

Step By Step Walkthrough

Using The Data Editor To Change Data Types

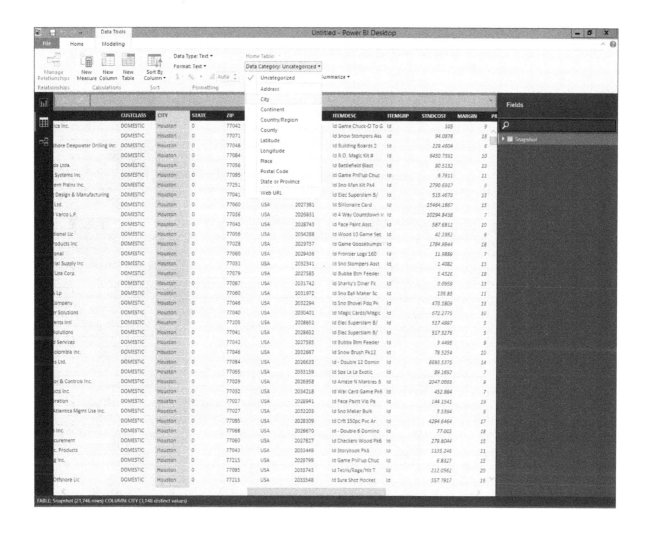

As you scroll through the data in the snapshot you will notice that there are a number of location specific fields there including the **CITY**, **STATE** etc. Power BI allows you to identify certain fields by their location type. If you select the **CITY** column and then select the **Data Category** dropdown list then you will be able to select the **City** Data Category. You can do the same for **STATE**, **ZIP**, and **COUNTRY**.

Step By Step Walkthrough

Using The Data Editor To Change Data Types

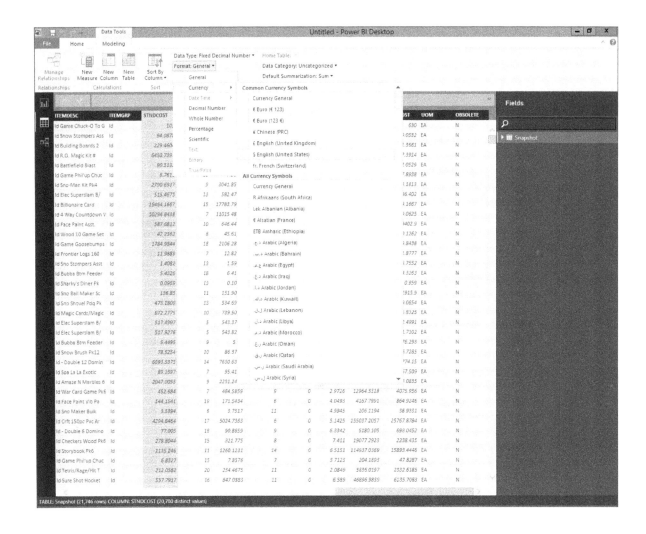

Finally there are a number of currency based fields in the dataset like **STDCOST** that you may want to format as currency fields. To do that just select the column, click on the **Format** dropdown list, select the **Currency** option and then select the **$ English (United States)** option.

Step By Step Walkthrough

Using The Data Editor To Change Data Types

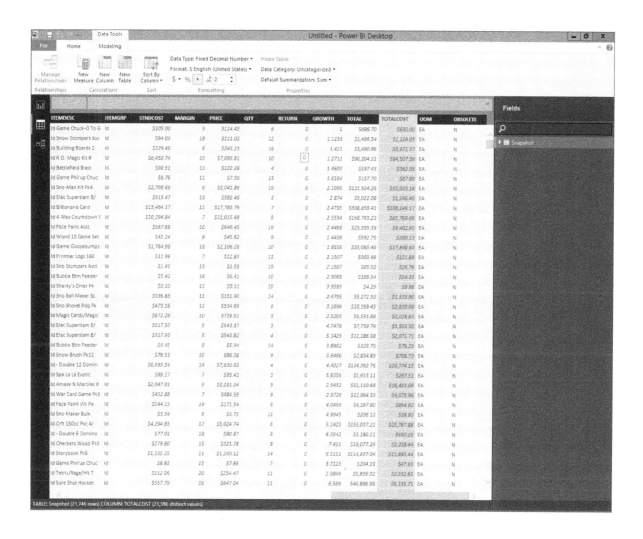

Now all of the data will be formatted just how we like it.

daxc
www.dynamicsaxcompanions.com
Dynamics AX Companions

- 213 -

www.blindsquirrelpublishing.com
© 2015 Blind Squirrel Publishing, LLC, All Rights Reserved

BLIND SQUIRREL
PUBLISHING

Saving The Dashboard Projects

Now that we have made a few changes to the data, we may want to save the project away.

Step By Step Walkthrough

Saving The Dashboard Projects

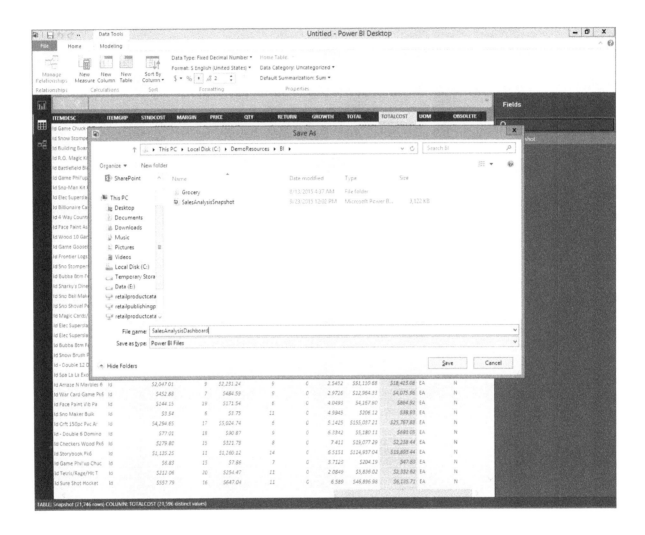

To save the project just click on the **Save** icon in the top left corner of the application, and when the **Save** dialog is displayed, give the project a file name and then click on the **Save** button.

daxc
www.dynamicsaxcompanions.com
Dynamics AX Companions
- 216 -
www.blindsquirrelpublishing.com
© 2015 Blind Squirrel Publishing, LLC, All Rights Reserved
BLIND SQUIRREL
PUBLISHING

Renaming Fields To Make Them More Friendly To The User

There is one last thing that we may want to do with our data before exiting from the **Data Editor** and that is to change the headings of the fields so that they are easier to read and also maybe a little more descriptive

Step By Step Walkthrough

Renaming Fields To Make Them More Friendly To The User

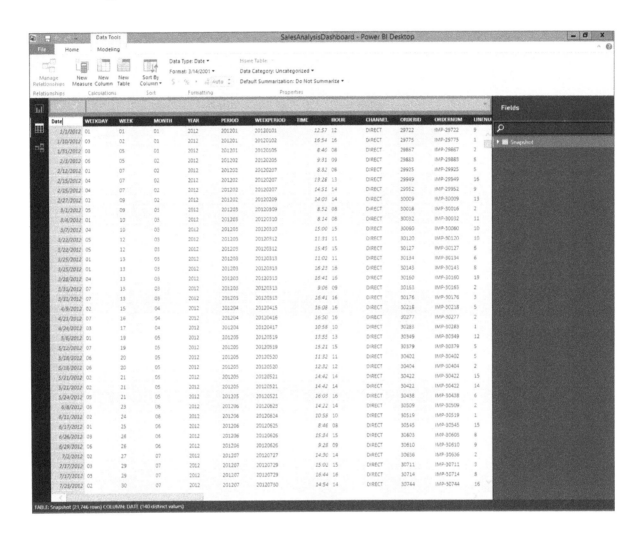

To change the heading all you need to do is click on the column heading and then change the name. For example, click on the **DATE** column and rename it to **Date**. Not a huge change but it does look tidier.

Step By Step Walkthrough

Renaming Fields To Make Them More Friendly To The User

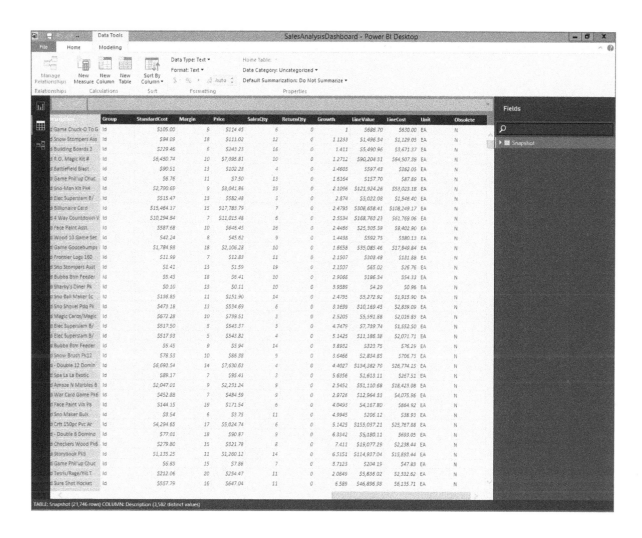

Now repeat that for all of the other columns and you are done.

Viewing The Changes In Query Editor

Now that we have made the changes, we will just atke a small detour and return to the **Query Editor** that we accessed in the previous section and see some of the changes that have been made.

Step By Step Walkthrough
Viewing The Changes In Query Editor

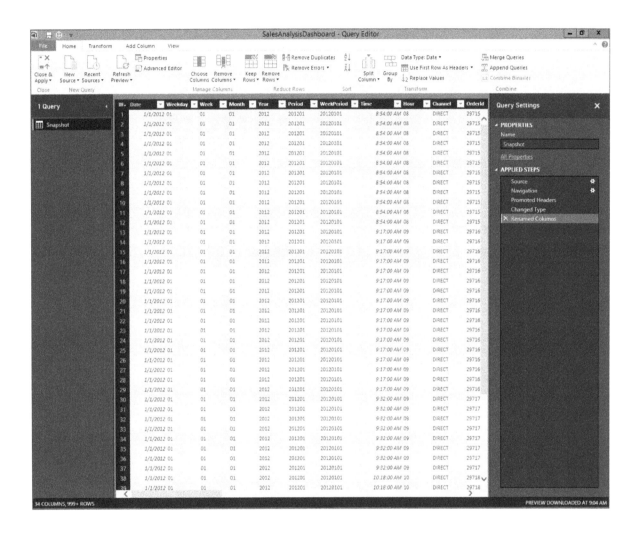

When you open up the **Query Editor** you will now see that there are some more changes listed in the **Applied Steps**.

da×c   www.dynamicsaxcompanions.com
Dynamics AX Companions
- 222 -
www.blindsquirrelpublishing.com
© 2015 Blind Squirrel Publishing, LLC , All Rights Reserved
BLIND SQUIRREL
PUBLISHING

Step By Step Walkthrough

Viewing The Changes In Query Editor

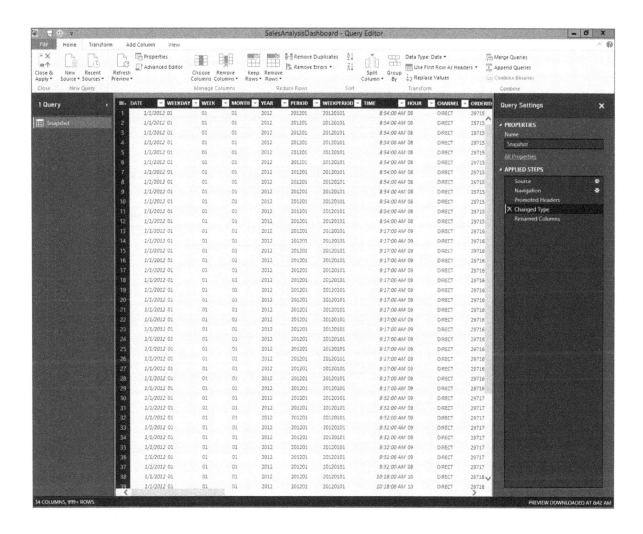

If you click on any of the prior steps you will see the data as it was at that time of the data transformation. The important point of this is that it shows how Power BI is building up the data from these steps so that when it refreshed the data then all of the steps are re-ran to get to the final data set.

Create More Detailed Dashboards

Now that we have massaged the data a little more we can try to build some more dashboards.

Step By Step Walkthrough

Create More Detailed Dashboards

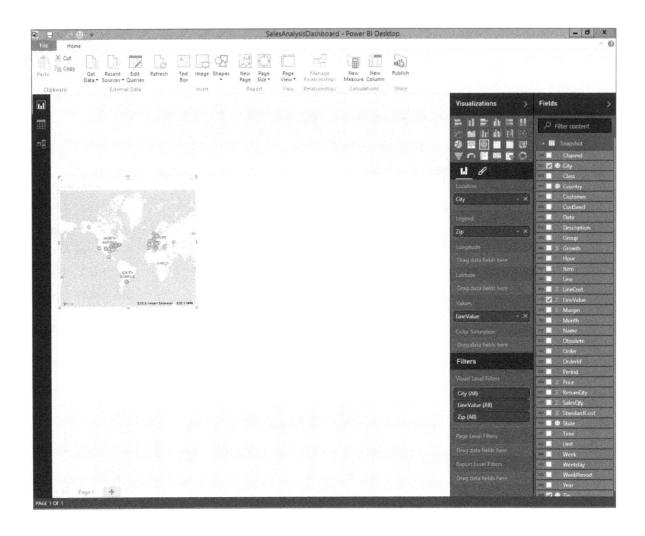

Click on the **Dashboard** icon on the left hand side to return to our initial dashboard that we created and you will see that it is still there even through we made changes to the data. What will look different will be all of the fields that are shown in the **Field Explorer** – they now look simpler.

Step By Step Walkthrough

Create More Detailed Dashboards

To create new dashboards all you need to do is click on the fields again and ass them to the canvas.

Publishing Dashboards to Power BI on Office365

Now that we have created our dashboards we can publish them back up to **Power BI** in **Office 365**. This will make them available to everyone in the organization and will also allow is to do some more clever things with the data.

Step By Step Walkthrough

Publishing Dashboards to Power BI on Office365

To publish the Dashboard that we just created to **Office 365** just click on the **Publish** button within the **Share** group of the **Home** ribbon bar, and when the confirmation dialog is displayed, click **Save**.

Step By Step Walkthrough

Publishing Dashboards to Power BI on Office365

The Desktop app will then connect to your **Office 365** account and publish the data up for you.

www.dynamicsaxcompanions.com
Dynamics AX Companions

- 231 -

www.blindsquirrelpublishing.com
© 2015 Blind Squirrel Publishing, LLC , All Rights Reserved

BLIND SQUIRREL
PUBLISHING

Step By Step Walkthrough

Publishing Dashboards to Power BI on Office365

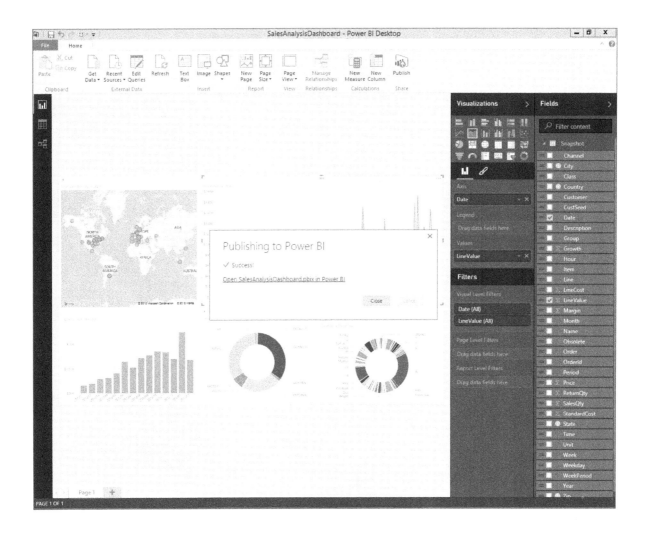

When everything is completed, you will get a cheery notice and then you can close out of the **Publishing** wizard.

Step By Step Walkthrough

Publishing Dashboards to Power BI on Office365

When you return to **Power BI** on **Office 365** then you will see that there is now a **Report** that looks exactly the same as the dashboard that you just designed.

daxc   www.dynamicsaxcompanions.com
        Dynamics AX Companions

- 233 -

        www.blindsquirrelpublishing.com
        © 2015 Blind Squirrel Publishing, LLC, All Rights Reserved

        BLIND SQUIRREL
        PUBLISHING

Creating a New Dashboard in Power BI Online

Power BI Online has one more additional feature that you can take advantage of and that is a concept of a **Dashboard**. Dashboards allow you to mash up data from multiple reports into one location that the user is then able to drill into, giving them one consolidated view.

Step By Step Walkthrough

Creating a New Dashboard in Power BI Online

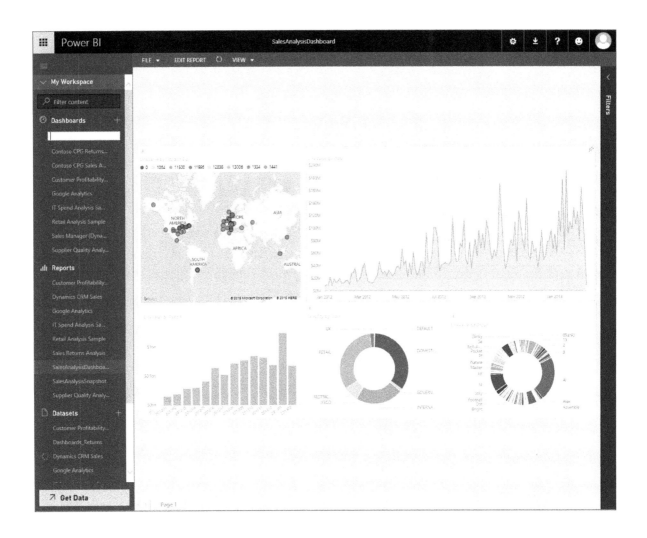

To create a new dashboard, just click on the + button beside the **Dashboards** group within Power BI.

Step By Step Walkthrough

Creating a New Dashboard in Power BI Online

Then type in name of the dashboard – for example **Contoso Sales Summary**.

Step By Step Walkthrough

Creating a New Dashboard in Power BI Online

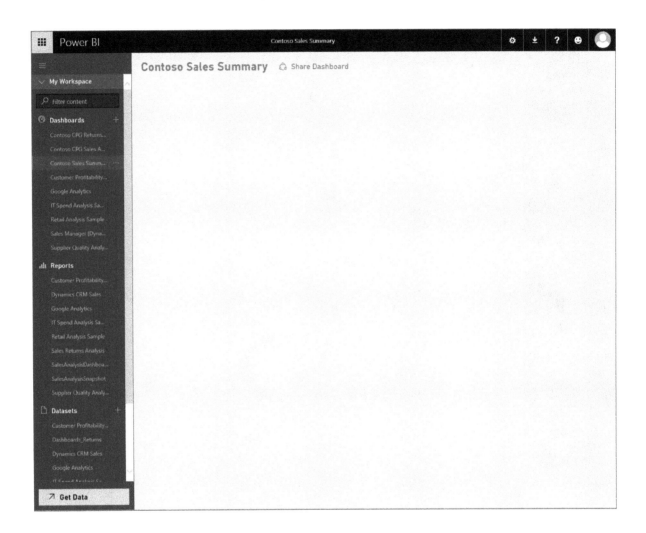

And you will be taken to a blank **Dashboard** canvas.

Pinning Report Tiles to Your Dashboards

Now that we have a **Dashboard** we can start populating it with data from our report. To do this we just find the report chart that we want and the pin it.

daxc

www.dynamicsaxcompanions.com
Dynamics AX Companions

- 239 -

www.blindsquirrelpublishing.com
© 2015 Blind Squirrel Publishing, LLC, All Rights Reserved

BLIND SQUIRREL
PUBLISHING

Step By Step Walkthrough

Pinning Report Tiles to Your Dashboards

So if you return back to the **SalesAnalysisDashboard** that was just imported, hover over any of the chart and you will notice that a pin shows up in the top right hand corner. All you need to do in order to add it to the dashboard is click on it.

Step By Step Walkthrough

Pinning Report Tiles to Your Dashboards

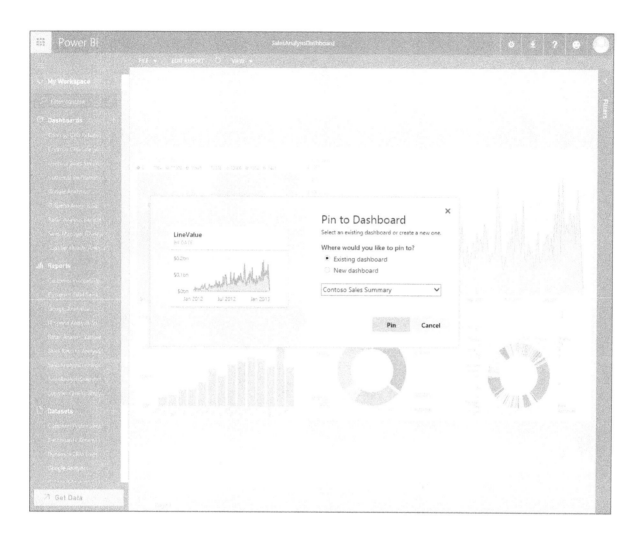

This will open up a dialog box asking you which **Dashboard** you want to pin it to and all you need to do is click on the **Pin** button.

daxc
www.dynamicsaxcompanions.com
Dynamics AX Companions
- 241 -
www.blindsquirrelpublishing.com
© 2015 Blind Squirrel Publishing, LLC , All Rights Reserved
BLIND SQUIRREL
PUBLISHING

Step By Step Walkthrough

Pinning Report Tiles to Your Dashboards

Power BI will tell you that the chart is now pinned to the Dashboard.

www.dynamicsaxcompanions.com
Dynamics AX Companions

- 242 -

www.blindsquirrelpublishing.com
© 2015 Blind Squirrel Publishing, LLC , All Rights Reserved

BLIND SQUIRREL
PUBLISHING

Step By Step Walkthrough

Pinning Report Tiles to Your Dashboards

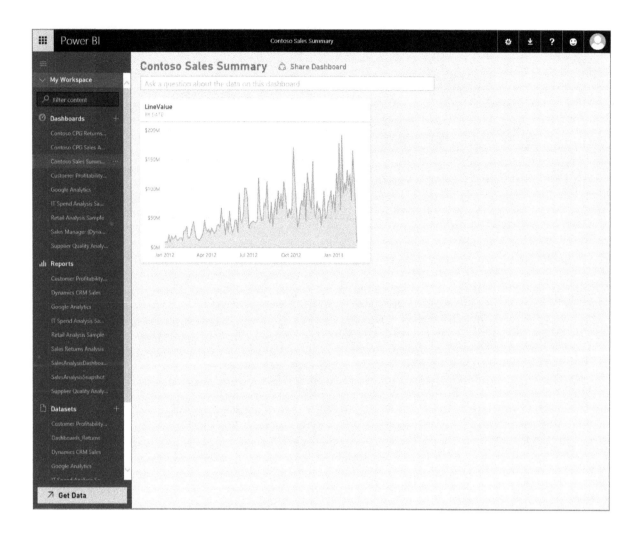

If you don't believe it then just click on the new **Dashboard** that you created and you will see it there.

Using Q&A to Build Dashboards Just By Asking for the Data

Power BI Online has one feature that is super cool and is not available within the Desktop version and that is the Q&A function. All you need to do to create a chart or query is to ask Power BI as a question.

Step By Step Walkthrough

Using Q&A to Build Dashboards Just By Asking for the Data

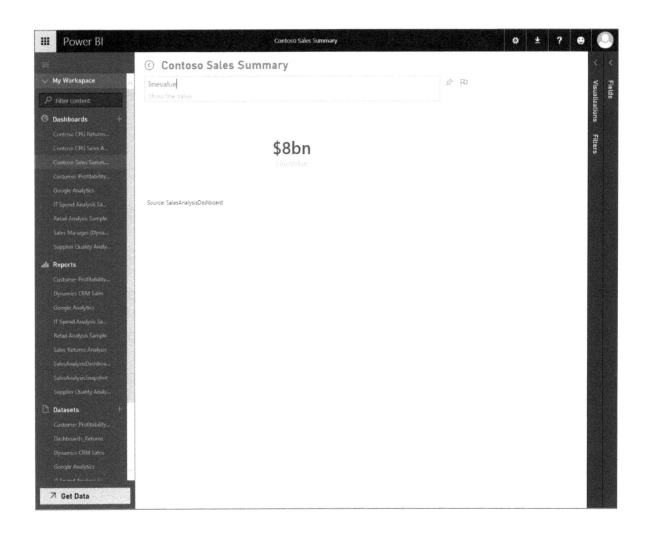

For example, if you just type in **LineValue** then you will get a total of all the **LineValue** fields in the data query that you created.

Step By Step Walkthrough

Using Q&A to Build Dashboards Just By Asking for the Data

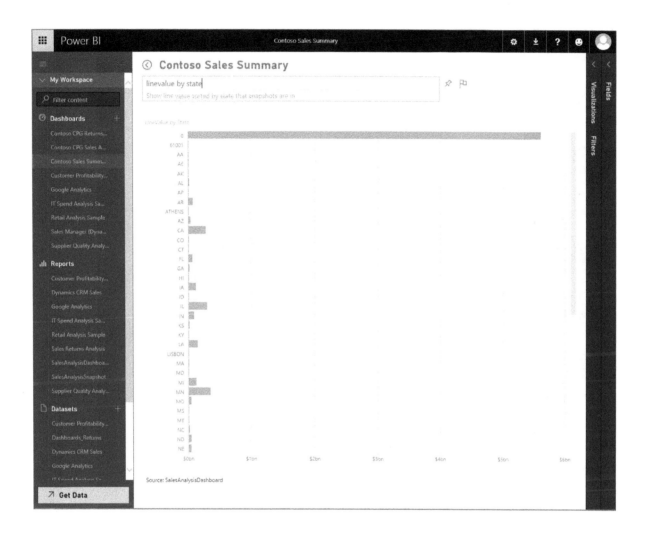

If you extend out the query to say **linevalue by state** then you will get all of the **LineValue** fields broken out by **State.**

Step By Step Walkthrough

Using Q&A to Build Dashboards Just By Asking for the Data

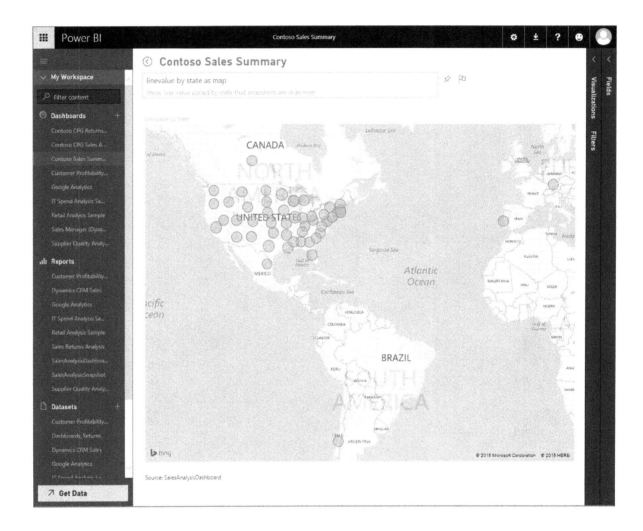

If you go one step further then you can add **as map** to the query and now it will show all of the sales by state on a map for you.

Using The Field Explorer To Help Find Data

You can gent even more elaborate with your queries by using more of the fields that you have defined in your query. All you need to know is what they are. To help you though there is a trick and that is to display the **Field Explorer**.

Step By Step Walkthrough

Using The Field Explorer To Help Find Data

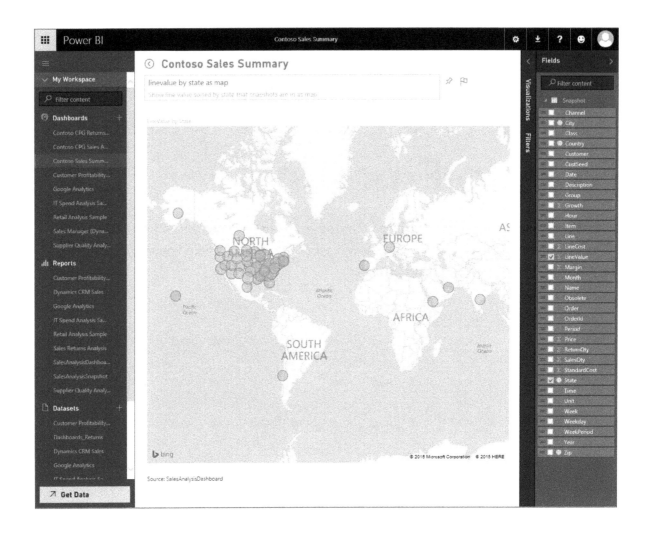

All you need to do is expand out the **Field Explorer** panel on the right hand side and you will see all of the fields with their default names.

www.dynamicsaxcompanions.com
Dynamics AX Companions
- 250 -
www.blindsquirrelpublishing.com
© 2015 Blind Squirrel Publishing, LLC , All Rights Reserved
BLIND SQUIRREL
PUBLISHING

Step By Step Walkthrough

Using The Field Explorer To Help Find Data

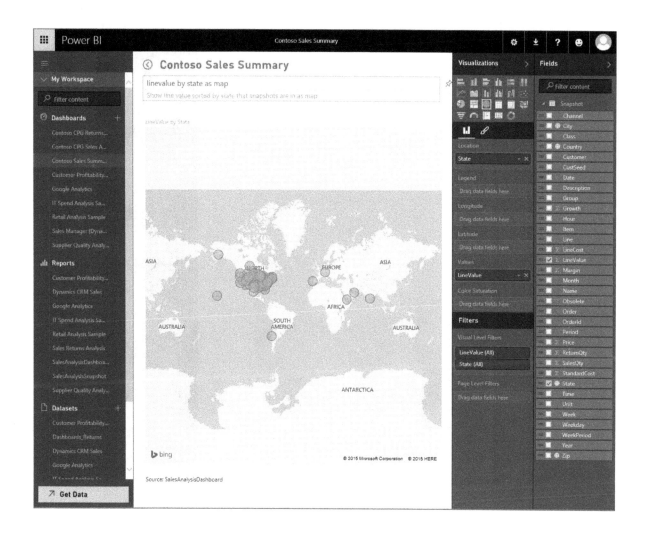

While you are doing that also expand out the **Visualizations** so that you can manually tweak the views if you like.

daxc   www.dynamicsaxcompanions.com
Dynamics AX Companions

- 251 -

www.blindsquirrelpublishing.com
© 2015 Blind Squirrel Publishing, LLC , All Rights Reserved

BLIND SQUIRREL
PUBLISHING

Step By Step Walkthrough

Using The Field Explorer To Help Find Data

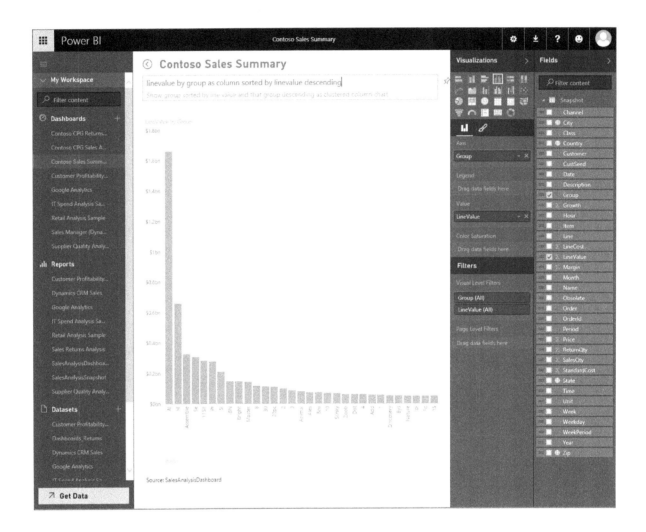

Now we can create a summary of all of the sales by product group in descending order just by asking **linevalue by group as columns sorted by linevalue descending**.

Step By Step Walkthrough

Using The Field Explorer To Help Find Data

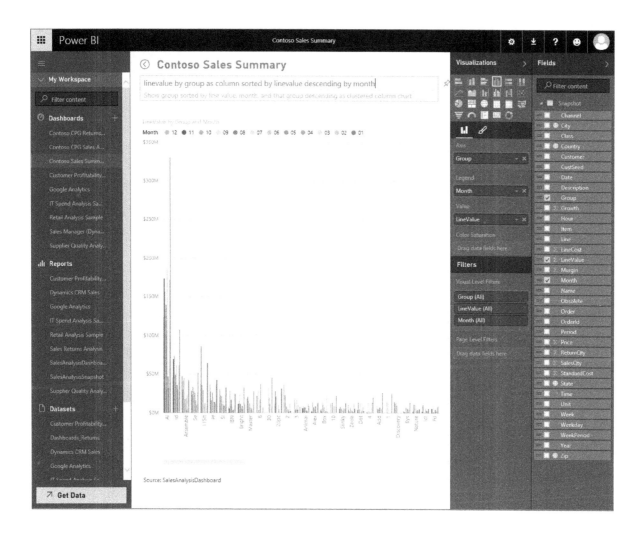

If we add in the **by month** then we also get all of the sales broken down further by month.

Step By Step Walkthrough

Using The Field Explorer To Help Find Data

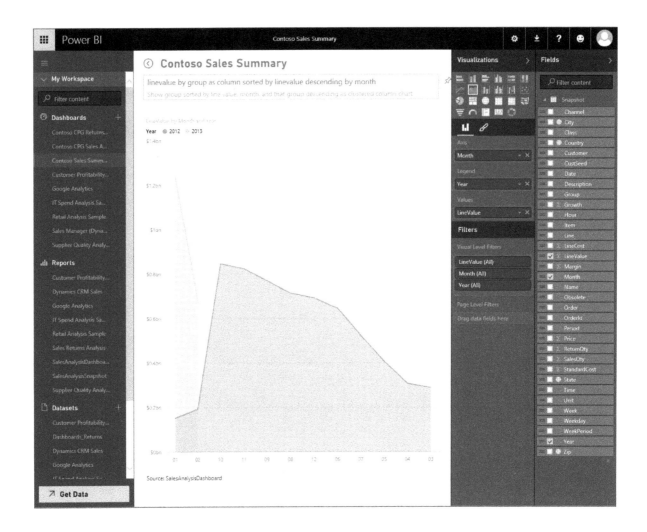

This is a little messy, so just change the visualization to a line area chart and it looks much nicer.

Step By Step Walkthrough

Using The Field Explorer To Help Find Data

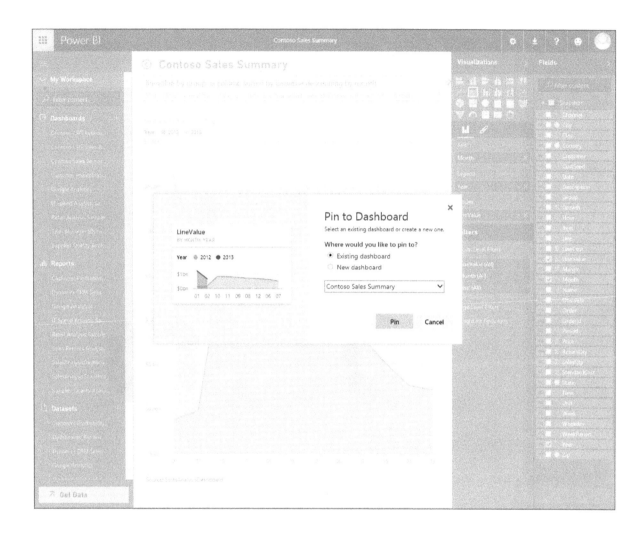

Now that we have the Q&A chart created and tweaked we can just click on the pin and add it to our dashboard.

Step By Step Walkthrough

Using The Field Explorer To Help Find Data

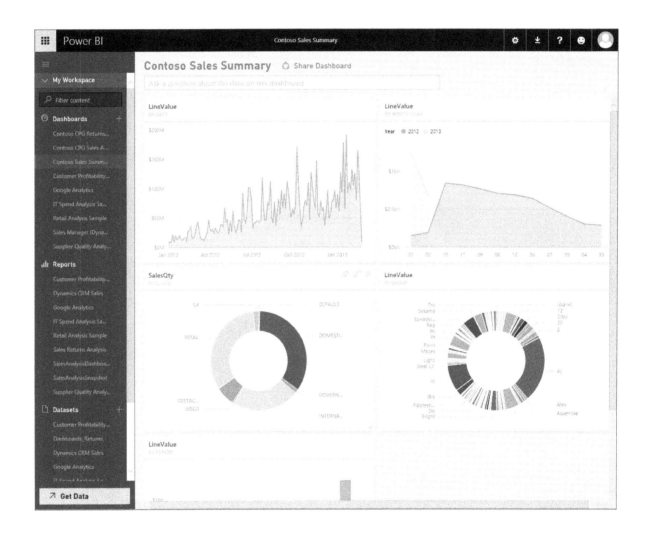

When we return to the dashboard we will now see the new chart is there for us to view even though it was never in our initial report that we created.

Downloading the Power BI Mobile App

You may think that this is more than enough BI options but there is one more way that we will look at our dashboards and that is through the free mobile app.

daxc
www.dynamicsaxcompanions.com
Dynamics AX Companions

- 257 -

www.blindsquirrelpublishing.com
© 2015 Blind Squirrel Publishing, LLC, All Rights Reserved

BLIND SQUIRREL
PUBLISHING

Step By Step Walkthrough

Downloading the Power BI Mobile App

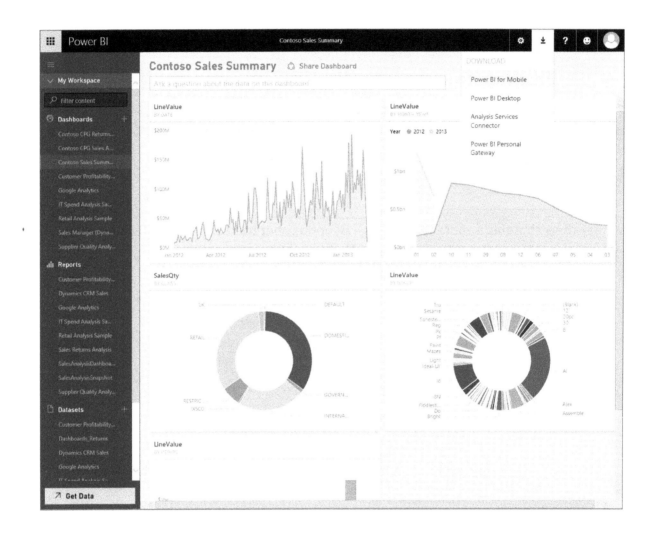

To get the Mobile App, all you need to do is click on the **Download** icon in the header of the **Power BI Online** workspace and click on the **Power BI Mobile** button.

Step By Step Walkthrough

Downloading the Power BI Mobile App

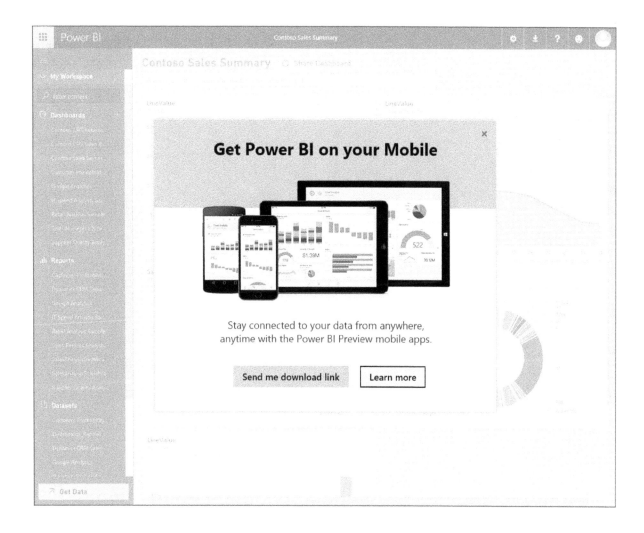

This will take you to an invitation page where you will be asked have the link e-mailed to you.

Step By Step Walkthrough

Downloading the Power BI Mobile App

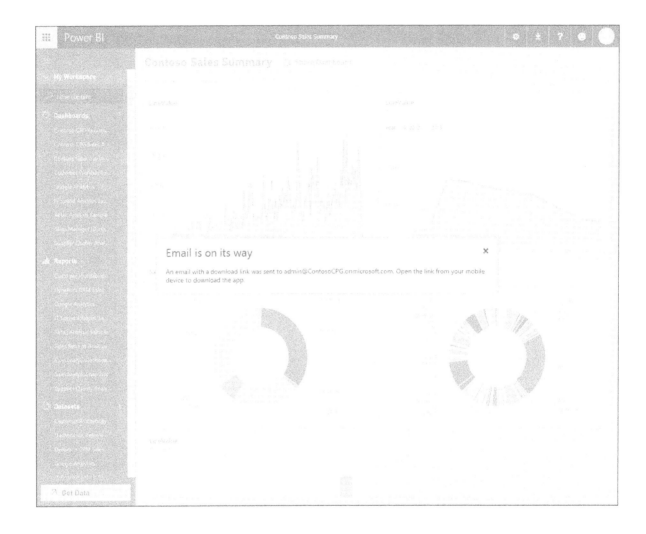

If you click on it then it will send the link to you and you can just download the app from there.

www.dynamicsaxcompanions.com
Dynamics AX Companions
- 260 -
www.blindsquirrelpublishing.com
© 2015 Blind Squirrel Publishing, LLC , All Rights Reserved
BLIND SQUIRREL
PUBLISHING

Step By Step Walkthrough

Downloading the Power BI Mobile App

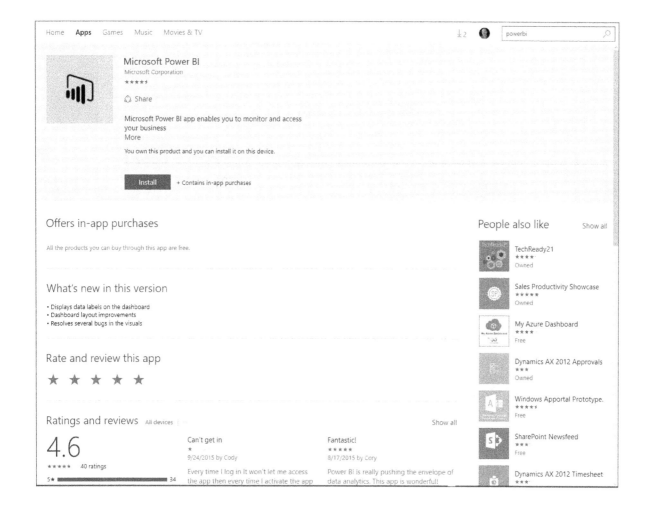

Alternatively if you just go to any of the app stores and do a search on **Power BI** then you will find the app there and you can just install it.

Connecting The Power BI Mobile App to Power BI Online

Once you have downloaded the Mobile App all you need to do is connect it up to your Power BI Online account and it will do all of the rest for you.

Step By Step Walkthrough

Connecting The Power BI Mobile App to Power BI Online

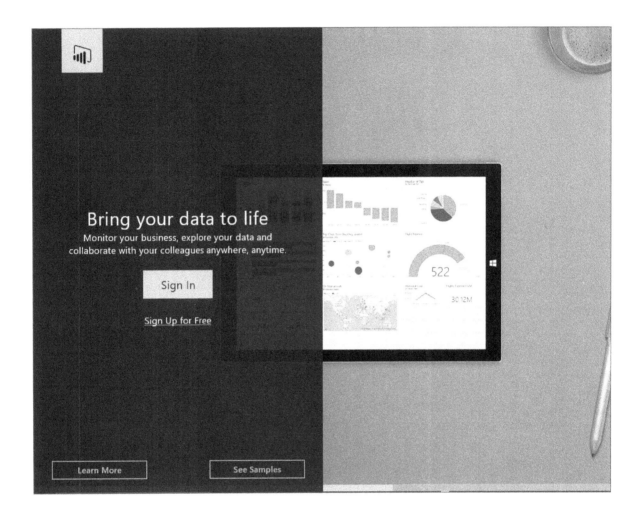

To connect the Mobile App up all you need to do is open it up and then click on the **Sign In** button.

Step By Step Walkthrough

Connecting The Power BI Mobile App to Power BI Online

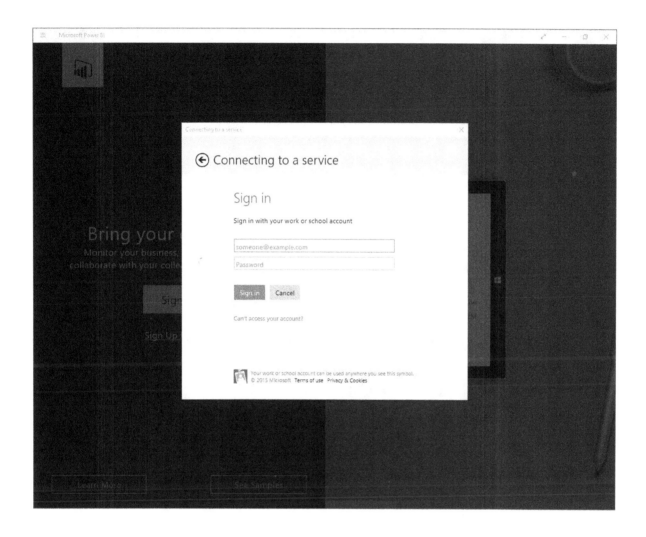

This will open up a Connection dialog and you just need to enter in the credentials that you use to log into your **O365** account and click on the **Sign In** button.

daxc
www.dynamicsaxcompanions.com
Dynamics AX Companions

- 265 -

www.blindsquirrelpublishing.com
© 2015 Blind Squirrel Publishing, LLC, All Rights Reserved

BLIND SQUIRREL
PUBLISHING

Step By Step Walkthrough

Connecting The Power BI Mobile App to Power BI Online

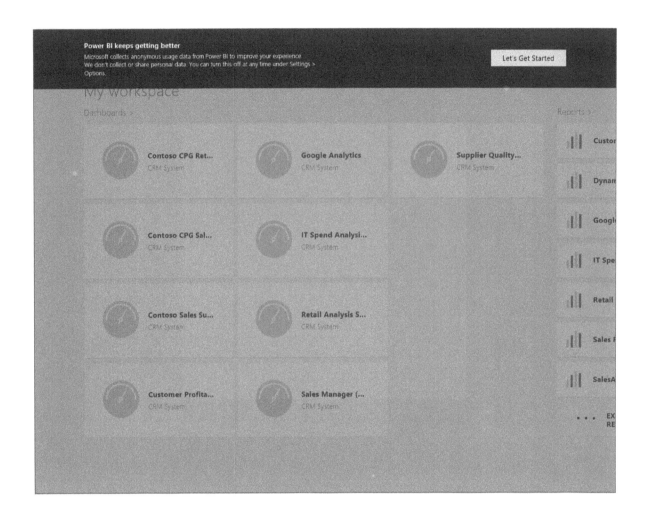

The Power BI Mobile App will then connect up and gather all of the dashboards that you have hosted on the server and make them available to you. All you need to do is click the **Lets Get Stated** button.

Step By Step Walkthrough

Connecting The Power BI Mobile App to Power BI Online

You will notice that the dashboard that we just created is immediately available to us and we can click on it.

daxc
www.dynamicsaxcompanions.com
Dynamics AX Companions
- 267 -
www.blindsquirrelpublishing.com
© 2015 Blind Squirrel Publishing, LLC , All Rights Reserved
BLIND SQUIRREL
PUBLISHING

Step By Step Walkthrough

Connecting The Power BI Mobile App to Power BI Online

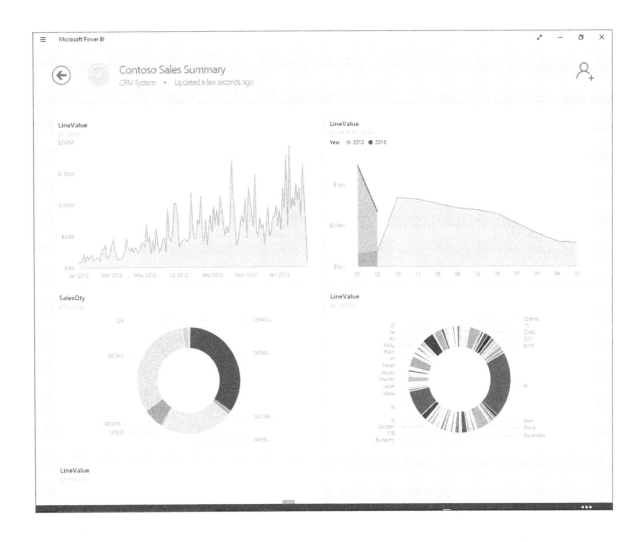

That will take us straight to the dashboard showing us all of the same data as we saw on-line.

www.dynamicsaxcompanions.com
Dynamics AX Companions

- 268 -

www.blindsquirrelpublishing.com
© 2015 Blind Squirrel Publishing, LLC, All Rights Reserved

BLIND SQUIRREL
PUBLISHING

Step By Step Walkthrough

Connecting The Power BI Mobile App to Power BI Online

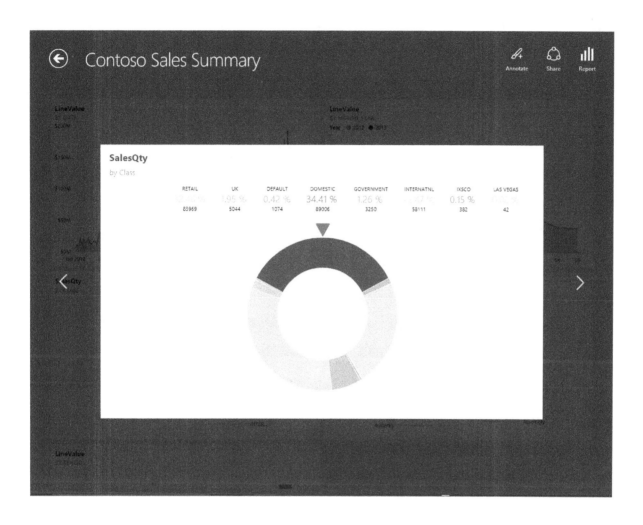

And if wee need more information then we can just drill into the report detail and also filter out the data.

daxc
www.dynamicsaxcompanions.com
Dynamics AX Companions

- 269 -

www.blindsquirrelpublishing.com
© 2015 Blind Squirrel Publishing, LLC, All Rights Reserved

BLIND SQUIRREL
PUBLISHING

Summary

In this presentation we have shown you how you can sign up for your very own Power BI hosted workspace, how you can download and use the **Desktop Designer** for free and create your own dashboards, and also how you can then publish those dashboards back up to Office 365 and Power BI online and further analyze the data. To make it even better all of this is then available through the Mobile application giving everyone access to your reports and dashboards even when they are on the go.

I think that this is enough excitement for this presentation, although make sure you all try this out. It is super cool and extremely useful to boot.

da𝑥c
www.dynamicsaxcompanions.com
Dynamics AX Companions
- 271 -
 BLIND SQUIRREL
PUBLISHING

CONCLUSION

This guide has been designed to show you how easy it is to start creating reports and dashboards directly from Dynamics AX and its data without breaking the bank and probably without having to spend any money either. Creating reports and dashboards is not something that requires IT to slave over tedious reporting structures – or at least for the simple reports that most users are asking for. They can be freed up to do other more exciting projects.

Also we tried to illustrate in this guide how the users are able to get the information that they want out of Dynamics AX themselves and also do it quickly with tools that they already know, and through new tools that they should be able to pick up really easily and become even better at sculpting their own data.

We have only scratched the surface on what you can do though with these tools. Once you have the data available as a user then you can manipulate it even more though the power of Excel, and also mine the data through the visualizations getting even more value out of this.

What are you all waiting for – start creating some reports already!

www.dynamicsaxcompanions.com
Dynamics AX Companions

- 273 -

www.blindsquirrelpublishing.com
© 2015 Blind Squirrel Publishing, LLC, All Rights Reserved

BLIND SQUIRREL
PUBLISHING

About The Author

Murray Fife is an Author of over 20 books on Microsoft Dynamics AX including the Bare Bones Configuration Guide series of over 15 books which step the user through the setup of initial Dynamics AX instance, then through the Financial modules and then through the configuration of the more specialized modules like production, service management, and project accounting. You can find all of his books on Amazon (www.amazon.com/author/murrayfife) and also even more on the BSP (www.blindsquirrelpublishing.com) site.

Murray is also the curator of the Dynamics AX Companions (www.dynamicsaxcompanions.com) site which he built from the ground up as a resource for all of the Dynamics AX community where you can find walkthroughs and blueprints that he created since first being introduced to the Dynamics AX product.

Throughout his 25+ years of experience in the software industry he has worked in many different roles during his career, including as a developer, an implementation consultant, a trainer and a demo guy within the partner channel which gives him a great understanding of the requirements for both customers and partner's perspective.

He is also a great supporter of the Dynamics AX community and has hosted scores webinars for the AX User Group (www.axug.com) and MS Dynamics World (www.msdynamicsworld.com), and has spoken at Microsoft Convergence and AXUG Summit conferences more times than he can count.

For more information on Murray, here is his contact information:

Email: murrayfife@dynamicsaxcompanions.com
Twitter: @murrayfife

Facebook: facebook.com/murraycfife
Google: google.com/+murrayfife
LinkedIn: linkedin.com/in/murrayfife

Blog: atinkerersnotebook.com
Docs: docs.com/mufife

Amazon: amazon.com/author/murrayfife

www.dynamicsaxcompanions.com
Dynamics AX Companions

- 275 -

www.blindsquirrelpublishing.com
© 2015 Blind Squirrel Publishing, LLC , All Rights Reserved

BLIND SQUIRREL
PUBLISHING

Need More Help with Dynamics AX

The Bare Bones Configuration Guides for Dynamics AX was developed to show you how to set up a company from the ground up and configure all of the common modules that most people would need, and a few that you might want to use.

It aims to demystify the setup process and prove that Dynamics AX is only as hard to configure as you make it, and if you are a mid-range customer that even you can get a company configured and working without turning on every bell and whistle and without breaking the bank.

There are 15 volumes in the current series and although each of these guides have been designed to stand by themselves as reference material for each of the modules within Dynamics AX, if they are taken as a whole series they are also a great training system that will allow even a novice on Dynamics AX work through the step by step instructions and build up a new company from scratch and learn a lot of the ins and outs of the system right away. The current guides are:

1. Configuring a Base Dynamics AX 2012 System
2. Configuring an Organization Within Dynamics AX 2012
3. Configuring The General Ledger Within Dynamics AX 2012
4. Configuring Cash And Bank Management Within Dynamics AX 2012
5. Configuring Accounts Receivable Within Dynamics AX 2012
6. Configuring Accounts Payable Within Dynamics AX 2012
7. Configuring Product Information Management Within Dynamics AX 2012
8. Configuring Inventory Management Within Dynamics AX 2012
9. Configuring Procurement & Sourcing Within Dynamics AX 2012
10. Configuring Sales Order Management Within Dynamics AX 2012
11. Configuring Human Resources Within Dynamics AX 2012
12. Configuring Project Management & Accounting Within Dynamics AX 2012
13. Configuring Production Control Within Dynamics AX 2012
14. Configuring Sales & Marketing Within Dynamics AX 2012
15. Configuring Service Management Within Dynamics AX 2012

If you are interested in finding out more about the series and also view all of the details including topics covered within the module then browse to the Bare Bones Configuration Guide landing page on the Dynamics AX Companions website. You will find all of the details, and also downloadable resources that help you with the setup of Dynamics AX. If you decipher the code in the signature at the bottom of this email then you can get 20% off the books. Here is the full link:

http://www.dynamicsaxcompanions.com/barebonesconfig

www.dynamicsaxcompanions.com
Dynamics AX Companions
- 277 -
www.blindsquirrelpublishing.com
© 2015 Blind Squirrel Publishing, LLC, All Rights Reserved
BLIND SQUIRREL
PUBLISHING

Usage Agreement

Murray Fife (the Author) agrees to grant, and the user of the eBook agrees to accept, a nonexclusive license to use the eBook under the terms and conditions of this eBook License Agreement ("Agreement"). Your use of the eBook constitutes your agreement to the terms and conditions set forth in this Agreement. This Agreement, or any part thereof, cannot be changed, waived, or discharged other than by a statement in writing signed by you and Murray Fife. Please read the entire Agreement carefully.

1. **EBook Usage.** The eBook may be used by one user on any device. The user of the eBook shall be subject to all of the terms of this Agreement, whether or not the user was the purchaser.

2. **Printing.** You may occasionally print a few pages of the eBook's text (but not entire sections), which may include sending the printed pages to a third party in the normal course of your business, but you must warn the recipient in writing that copyright law prohibits the recipient from redistributing the eBook content to anyone else. Other than the above, you may not print pages and/or distribute eBook content to others.

3. **Copyright, Use and Resale Prohibitions.** The Author retains all rights not expressly granted to you in this Agreement. The software, content, and related documentation in the eBook are protected by copyright laws and international copyright treaties, as well as other intellectual property laws and treaties. Nothing in this Agreement constitutes a waiver of the author's rights. The Author will not be responsible for performance problems due to circumstances beyond its reasonable control. Other than as stated in this Agreement, you may not copy, print, modify, remove, delete, augment, add to, publish, transmit, sell, resell, license, create derivative works from, or in any way exploit any of the eBook's content, in whole or in part, in print or electronic form, and you may not aid or permit others to do so. The unauthorized use or distribution of copyrighted or other proprietary content is illegal and could subject the purchaser to substantial damages. Purchaser will be liable for any damage resulting from any violation of this Agreement.

4. **No Transfer.** This license is not transferable by the eBook purchaser unless such transfer is approved in advance by the Author.

5. **Disclaimer.** The eBook, or any support given by the Author are in no way substitutes for assistance from legal, tax, accounting, or other qualified professionals. If legal advice or other expert assistance is required, the services of a competent professional person should be sought.

6. **Limitation of Liability.** The eBook is provided "as is" and the Author does not make any warranty or representation, either express or implied, to the eBook, including its quality, accuracy, performance, merchantability, or fitness for a particular purpose. You assume the entire risk as to the results and performance of the eBook. The Author does not warrant, guarantee, or make any representations regarding the use of, or the results obtained with, the eBook in terms of accuracy, correctness or reliability. In no event will the Author be liable for indirect, special, incidental, or consequential damages arising out of delays, errors, omissions, inaccuracies, or the use or inability to use the eBook, or for interruption of the eBook, from whatever cause. This will apply even if the Author has been advised that the possibility of such damage exists. Specifically, the Author is not responsible for any costs, including those incurred as a result of lost profits or revenue, loss of data, the cost of recovering such programs or data, the cost of any substitute program, claims by third parties, or similar costs. Except for the Author's indemnification obligations in Section 7.2, in no case will the Author's liability exceed the amount of license fees paid.

7. **Hold Harmless / Indemnification.**
7.1 You agree to defend, indemnify and hold the Author and any third party provider harmless from and against all third party claims and damages (including reasonable attorneys' fees) regarding your use of the eBook, unless the claims or damages are due to the Author's or any third party provider's gross negligence or willful misconduct or arise out of an allegation for which the Author is obligated to indemnify you.
7.2. The Author shall defend, indemnify and hold you harmless at the Author's expense in any suit, claim or proceeding brought against you alleging that your use of the eBook delivered to you hereunder directly infringes a United States patent, copyright, trademark, trade secret, or other third party proprietary right, provided the Author is (i) promptly notified, (ii) given the assistance required at the Author's expense, and (iii) permitted to retain legal counsel of the Author's choice and to direct the defense. The Author also agrees to pay any damages and costs awarded against you by final judgment of a court of last resort in any such suit or any agreed settlement amount on account of any such alleged infringement, but the Author will have no liability for settlements or costs incurred without its consent. Should your use of any such eBook be enjoined, or in the event that the Author desires to minimize its liability hereunder, the Author will, at its option and expense, (i) substitute a fully equivalent non-infringing eBook for the infringing item; (ii) modify the infringing item so that it no longer infringes but remains substantially equivalent; or (iii) obtain for you the right to continue use of such item. If none of the foregoing is feasible, the Author will terminate your access to the eBook and refund to you the applicable fees paid by you for the infringing item(s). THE FOREGOING STATES THE ENTIRE LIABILITY OF THE AUTHOR AND YOUR SOLE REMEDY FOR INFRINGEMENT OR FOR ANY BREACH OF WARRANTY OF NON-INFRINGEMENT, EXPRESS OR IMPLIED. THIS INDEMNITY WILL NOT APPLY TO ANY ALLEGED INFRINGEMENT BASED UPON A COMBINATION OF OTHER SOFTWARE OR INFORMATION WITH THE EBOOK WHERE THE EBOOK WOULD NOT HAVE OTHERWISE INFRINGED ON ITS OWN.

www.ingramcontent.com/pod-product-compliance
Lightning Source LLC
Chambersburg PA
CBHW080358060326
40689CB00019B/4056